D1379579

curriculum connections

Peoples of the East, Southeast, and Plains

BROWN
BEAR
BOOKS

Published by Brown Bear Books Limited

An imprint of:
The Brown Reference Group Ltd
68 Topstone Road
Redding
Connecticut 06896
USA
www.brownreference.com

© 2009 The Brown Reference Group Ltd

ISBN: 978-1-933834-77-1

Editorial Director: Lindsey Lowe
Senior Managing Editor: Tim Cooke
Managing Editor: Laura Durman
Editor: Clare Collinson
Designer: Rob Norridge
Picture Researcher: Clare Collinson

Library of Congress Cataloging-in-Publication Data available upon request

36242060385883

Picture Credits

Cover Image
Jupiter Images/photos.com

George Catlin/Library of Congress: p.91; Edward S. Curtis/Library of Congress: p.30, p.34, p.41, p.103; M. J. Danforth/Library of Congress: p.60; William Emmons/Library of Congress: p.94; Jeffrey J. Frank/Shutterstock: p.66; F. W. Greenough/Library of Congress: p.25; Kavram/Shutterstock: p.20; Library of Congress: p.18, p.69; p.89; Louisiana Purchase Exposition Co./Library of Congress: p.11; McKenney & Hall/Library of Congress: p.51, p.87; Christopher Meder Photography/Shutterstock: p.57; Photos.com/Jupiterimages Corporation: p.27, p.37, p.48, p.72, p.98, p.102; F.A. Rinehart/Library of Congress: p.13, p.15; Aaron Rutton/Shutterstock: p.21; Nancy Catherine Walker/Shutterstock: p.63.

Artwork © The Brown Reference Group Ltd

The Brown Reference Group Ltd has made every effort to trace copyright holders of the pictures used in this book. Anyone having claims to ownership not identified above is invited to contact The Brown Reference Group Ltd.

Printed in the United States of America

Contents

Introduction

Native North Americans forms part of the Curriculum Connections project. The six volumes of the set cover all aspects of the history and culture of native peoples in what are now the United States and Canada. Each volume covers a particular aspect of Native American life: Peoples of the East, Southeast, and Plains; Peoples of the Southwest, West, and North; Arts, Society, and Religion; History; Personalities and Places; and Warfare, Economy, and Technology.

About this set

Each volume in *Native North Americans* features a series of articles arranged in A–Z order. The articles are all listed in the contents pages of each book, and can also be located through the indexes.

Each illustrated article provides a concise but accurate summary of its subject, accompanied where relevant by informative maps. Articles about major tribes are each accompanied by a fact file that provides a summary of essential information.

Within each article, two key aids to learning are located in sidebars in the margins of each page:

Curriculum Context sidebars indicate that a subject has particular relevance to state and national American history guidelines and curricula. They highlight essential information or suggest useful ways for students to include a subject in their studies.

Glossary sidebars define key words within the text.

At the end of the book, a summary Glossary lists the key terms defined in the volume. There is also a list of further print and Web-based resources and a full volume index.

About this volume

This book studies the various native peoples who inhabited the eastern part of North America: the Atlantic coast from the Saint Lawrence River south to Florida, the Eastern Woodlands, and the Plains in the heart of the continent, beyond the Ohio and Mississippi Valleys. This was the region where the first settled societies emerged in North America— including the mound-building peoples known as the Mississippians—and also where native groups had some of the earliest sustained contact with Europeans. Consequently, the book covers some of the peoples whose names are still familiartoday, such as the Arapaho, the Cherokee, and the Comanche. Some were on friendly terms with the newcomers, such as the confederacy the English called the "Five Civilized Tribes." Others, such as the Iroquois or the Powhatan, were more inclined to resist the new arrivals.

The eastern half of the United States includes a range of landscapes that shaped how their inhabitants lived. The people covered in this book included farmers of the plains but also hunters and gatherers from the woodlands. Some lived in the potentially cold climate of northeast Canada; others lived in the semi-tropical climate of Florida. The ways in which each people adapted to their own local environment is just one of the fascinating topics for study you'll discover in this book.

Adena and Hopewell

The Adena Pre-Contact people (700–100 BCE) lived along the Ohio River Valley. They were named for the modern city near their main settlement. The Hopewell Pre-Contact group came after the Adena and survived until about 500 CE. The Hopewell were influential throughout the northeastern Woodland and along the Mississippi River into the Midwest.

The Adena and Hopewell are both remembered for their complex burial customs and huge geometrical earthworks. These earthworks can still be seen today.

The Adena

The Adena were hunter–gatherers, catching animals and collecting wild plants to live on. They also grew a few crops, such as pumpkins and sunflowers.

The Adena people built clusters of burial mounds that contained the bodies of important people and their closest followers. These graves were often filled with funeral offerings. The mounds were cone shaped, and, typically, one mound rose above another as new burials were made. Some of the mounds reached as high as 70 feet (23 m). A group of several mounds was usually surrounded by an earth bank up to 500 feet (150 m) across. One of the largest was Grave Creek Mound in West Virginia.

The Adena lived in circular thatched huts with walls made of wattle (a mixture of mud and straw) that were built around a central fireplace. Their crafts included making pottery jars and bowls and carved stone pipes.

The Hopewell

By about 200 CE the Adena were declining in importance and had been replaced by the Hopewell, who were a similar but more advanced group. The Hopewell were

Hunter–gatherers
People who obtain most of their food by hunting wild animals and eating plants gathered from the wild.

Curriculum Context
Many curricula ask students to trace the rise of diverse cultures from hunter–gatherers to farmers.

named for the modern-day owner of one of the group's main sites in the Ohio River Valley.

The Hopewell were a highly religious people. They were also great traders with a trade network extending far beyond their main homeland, bringing in raw materials for artists and craftspeople to make objects to be used as offerings at burials. They did everything on a greater scale than the Adena. Their burial mounds could reach up to 140 feet (40 m) high, and the surrounding earthworks extended for miles in geometrical patterns. The size of the mounds suggests that the Hopewell had a powerful ruling class.

The best memorial to Adena–Hopewell skill and organization survives in the Serpent Mound in Ohio. It curls along a natural ridge for over 400 yards (430 m).

A declining culture

By the end of the fifth century CE the Hopewell were in decline. The reasons for this are unclear, but some archeologists believe that the Hopewell civilization ended because of overpopulation, food shortages, and the breakdown of the group's trade network. In the 19th century many white settlers considered their earthworks to be far beyond the abilities of Native Americans, crediting them to a mythical, vanished people.

Curriculum context

Students learning about Pre-Contact societies might be asked to describe the rise and decline of mound-building cultures.

The Hopewell trade network

Enormous quantities of funerary objects were needed as offerings at Hopewell burials, so a trade network was established to bring in raw materials for Hopewell artists and craftspeople. Traders brought in obsidian (a natural type of glass produced by cooling lava) from the Rocky Mountains and copper from the Great Lakes. Artists used silver from Canada, and mica (a mineral that breaks easily into thin slices) and clay from the Appalachian Mountains. The objects they produced are among the finest of any Pre-Contact group.

Algonquian

The Algonquian were made up of independent nomadic hunting groups who lived along the upper tributaries of the Ottawa and Gatineau rivers in Quebec, Canada. The Algonquian hunting groups joined together in the summer along rivers to fish and socialize. In the winter the same groups separated into smaller camps and hunted.

Curriculum Context

Attitudes toward nature are an important part of understanding a Native American society. The Algonquian believed that all creatures were part of a natural cycle of life and death.

For most of the year it was a harsh existence, and starvation was always a threat. In response to these conditions the Algonquian developed three basic principles that governed their lives. The first principle was the individual right of dignity, by which no one person could decide the fate of another. For example, family feuds were resolved by the families involved, not by a tribal council. The second was the sharing of supplies and resources, which meant that the more scarce food became, the more readily it was shared. Third was a belief that all creatures, including humans, were part of a natural cycle. In life humans ate other animals, but in death humans were returned to the earth to provide nourishment to the plants on which other animals depended.

Besides hunting and trapping, the Algonquian built birchbark canoes. These canoes could travel great distances along the Ottawa and St. Lawrence rivers, enabling the Algonquian to trade with other tribes.

Trade with European settlers

At the beginning of the 17th century Algonquian expertise in hunting and transport attracted the attention of white fur traders. These skills were to prove a mixed blessing, since the Algonquian, and many other Native American groups, became involved in the scramble to provide fur pelts—especially beaver—for a rapidly growing European market.

Algonquian at war

During the latter part of the 18th century the Algonquian found themselves embroiled in bloody conflicts involving the French, the British, the Dutch, and other European nations, all trying to gain control of the fur trade. The white settlers formed alliances with various Native American groups, supplying opposing tribes with firearms and other weapons.

Tribal conflicts

The influx of European weaponry intensified the wars that had been fought between the groups. For example, the Algonquian, supplied with French weapons, fought against the Iroquoian-speaking Mohawk and the Oneida, who in turn were backed by the Dutch. The result was that all the Native American peoples suffered: They lost many lives and exhausted their supplies of fur from forest animals.

Curriculum Context

The cooperation that existed in the 1700s between colonists and Native American societies is often as significant as the conflict between them.

Algonquian

Language:	Algonquian
Area:	Along the Gatineau and Ottawa rivers in Canada
Reservation:	Quebec, Ontario
Population:	Approximately 2,000 today
Housing:	Villages of cone-shaped tepees, wigwams, and rectangular houses
European contact:	French trader Samuel de Champlain in 1603
Neighbors:	Other Algonquian-speaking peoples; also Iroquois peoples who were their enemy
Lifestyle:	Hunting, fishing, and gathering wild food
Food:	Game, fish, and berries
Crafts:	Decorating clothing with beading and porcupine quills; wood carving

As well as conflict over trade the French and British were involved in a bitter struggle over territory. This European dispute lasted, on and off, from 1689 until the late 18th century. By 1763, with the end of what is known as the French and Indian War (1754–1763), the French, having lost, were forced to forfeit their claim to much of the Northeast.

The Algonquian were left at the mercy of the British, who forced them into a life of poverty and hardship. Today the number of Algonquian people is about 2,000, yet they are one of the few tribes that have remained in their original homeland, Ontario.

Algonquian speakers

The Algonquian language is the most common Native American language in North America. It spawned about 50 related but distinct languages spoken by hundreds of tribes. The Algonquian-speaking group originated in the Woodland region, including the Great Lakes, New England, and Virginia. The language spread as far as the southern Plains when the Cheyenne settled there.

Many Algonquian words have passed into the English language. Some examples are chipmunk, opossum, raccoon, tomahawk, moccasin, squash, wigwam, and Connecticut, which means "long river."

The Algonquian name

Historians disagree about the origin of the name Algonquian (or Algonkin). The most likely possibility is that "Algonquian," as applied to the tribal groups, originally stems from the Maliseet word *a'legonka*, meaning "dancers." In 1603 a French explorer and fur trader, Samuel de Champlain, was invited to a feast hosted by three tribes—the Maliseet (or Etchemin), Montagnais, and another Algonquian-speaking group—who were celebrating a victory over their longtime enemies, the Iroquois. Legend has it that Champlain mistook the Algonquian word for "dancers" for the name of the third tribe, now known as Algonquian.

Arapaho

The Arapaho, according to legend, originally came from the headwaters of the Mississippi River near Lake Superior. They planted corn and lived in villages. Later, according to other legends, they "lost the corn," meaning that they stopped farming and became hunters.

In the early 18th century the Arapaho traveled to the plains and prairies of what are now eastern North Dakota and western Minnesota. There they hunted buffalo and lived in tepees. In time the group became great traders, buying and selling horses and tanned hides to other Native Americans.

The name Arapaho comes from the Pawnee word *tirapihu* or *larapihu*, meaning "he buys or trades." The Arapaho call themselves *Invna-ina*, meaning "people of our own kind." Their allies the Cheyenne knew them as *Hitaniwo'iv* ("cloud men").

A tribe divided
The Arapaho speak an Algonquian language similar to that of the Gros Ventre. In fact, the two groups speak

Tepee
A cone-shaped tent built with a pole framework traditionally covered with animal skins.

A group of Arapaho, photographed in 1904, outside a tepee surrounded by a brush fence.

dialects of a single variant that differs greatly from other Algonquian languages. It is possible that the Arapaho and the Gros Ventre once belonged to a single group.

In the early 19th century the Arapaho divided into southern and northern groups. Those who moved south into eastern Colorado became known as the Southern Arapaho.

The Southern Arapaho lived on the plains of eastern Colorado until white settlers began to disrupt their way of life. The settlers spread diseases, such as whooping cough and measles, among the Arapaho and other Native Americans and drove away their game. Then gold was discovered on the banks of the South Platte River in Colorado, and by 1858 white gold prospectors had begun to flood into Arapaho lands.

Removal from homelands

The U.S. government tried to force the Arapaho and the Cheyenne onto a reservation. At first the groups refused to go, but later they agreed. However, despite the agreement, on November 29, 1864, U.S. troops carried out a massacre of Chief Black Kettle's Cheyenne at Sand Creek, killing some 400 men, women, and children. On October 28, 1867, Chief Little Raven of the Southern Arapaho signed the Medicine Lodge Treaty in Kansas with the U.S. government, agreeing to move to the Indian Territory. The treaty was also agreed to by the Comanche, Kiowa, and Southern Cheyenne.

Reservations and a new life

Under the terms of the Medicine Lodge Treaty, the various tribes were to be confined to several reservations. The U.S. authorities, attempting to undermine the groups' cultures, built white-run schools on the reservations and instructed the Native Americans in European-style agriculture.

Curriculum Context

The spread of European diseases among Native Americans is an obvious aspect of the natural interaction between the "Old and "New" worlds after 1492.

Indian Territory

Land mainly in present-day Oklahoma set aside in 1834 for Native Americans who had been forced to leave their homelands. The Indian Territory was dissolved when Oklahoma became a state in 1907.

From 1874 to 1875 the Cheyenne, Comanche, and Kiowa rebelled against the government, but the Arapaho refused to join their revolt. The Arapaho remained loyal to the Medicine Lodge Treaty, even though the tribe was suffering severe poverty.

Ghost Dance religion

In the late 19th century the Arapaho became involved in the Ghost Dance religion. Among other things, members of this religion believed that a messiah would come to unite all Native Americans. During the dance the dancers worked themselves into a frenzy. The religion died away, however, soon after the massacre at Wounded Knee of Sioux who had fled Pine Ridge Reservation following the killing of Sitting Bull.

Arapaho today

In 1890 the Arapaho and the Cheyenne sold a large section of their reservation to the United States. In 1907 however, Oklahoma became a state, and the Indian Territory was dissolved. The Arapaho population declined in the early 20th century, reaching a low point in the 1920s. Today there are an estimated 2,000 living on a reservation in Wyoming and 3,000 in Oklahoma.

Ghost Dance
Native American religious movement of the late 19th century that involved the performance of a ritual dance in order to bring an end to the westward expansion of white settlers and restore Native American land and traditional tribal life.

This photograph, taken in 1899, shows an Arapaho woman wearing traditional dress decorated with rows of elk's teeth.

Assiniboine

The Assiniboine come from western Saskatchewan, Canada. Europeans thought the area to be too wild to be inhabited, but it had been occupied by many Native American groups for generations. The Assiniboine had managed to survive the cold winters there by hunting buffalo and other game. During the late 18th and early 19th centuries, bands of Assiniboine moved south into U.S. territory, to what is now Montana.

Hudson's Bay Company

A trading company set up in 1670 in the Hudson Bay area of North America. It controlled the fur trade in the region for centuries, forming a network of trading posts and obtaining fur from local peoples in exchange for goods shipped from Britain.

Western bands of the Assiniboine were first visited by a trader from the Hudson's Bay Company, Henry Kelsey, in the late 1600s. In 1731 a French-Canadian explorer, La Verendreye, accompanied eastern Assiniboine on a trade expedition to the Mandan people, who lived in villages along the Upper Missouri River. This area later became an important center for trade between the Native American groups of the northern Plains and the European settlers.

The Assiniboine entered into an alliance with the Cree, Ojibway, and Monsoni to warn off the Sioux, Arikara, Cheyenne, Blackfoot, and Gros Ventre.

Trading with settlers

The Assiniboine at first traded with the Hudson's Bay Company but then began to deal more with French traders from Quebec. As competition for trade routes along the river increased, the Assiniboine played one party off against another. Sometimes they attacked European merchants and sometimes other northern Plains peoples. The Assiniboine became powerful in the area, but later they were undermined by major smallpox epidemics. The worst epidemic occurred in 1840, when 75 percent of the population died.

During the 19th century the Assiniboine signed treaties with white traders allowing trading posts to be built on their lands. In 1828 the American Fur Company began building Fort Union, which became a major center for Assiniboine trade.

Improved forms of transportation, such as steamboats and railroads, brought white immigrants to the region. Most of these white settlers were lured to the region by wild tales of gold found on the Plains.

Land disputes

By the mid-19th century Canadian government legislation had forced groups in the Montana–Saskatchewan area to define their boundaries. Many treaties and agreements tried to do this, but mistakes were often made. For example, land allotted to the Assiniboine was later given to the Blackfoot. This caused much hostility between the two groups, who were old enemies, and eventually the Assiniboine, together with their allies the Cree, drove the Blackfoot out of western Saskatchewan.

By the end of the 19th century there were no more buffalo left in the region, and hundreds of Assiniboine had starved to death. The surviving Assiniboine were moved by the U.S. and Canadian governments onto reservations in Montana and Alberta.

This photograph taken in 1898 shows the Assiniboine chief Wets It wearing a horn headdress.

Blackfoot

The Blackfoot were originally from the Great Lakes region but drifted westward over time to the northern Plains. There they acquired guns from the French and English in the east and horses from the Spanish in the south. They settled in Montana and Alberta in the mid-18th century, dominating the territory.

Curriculum Context

Many curricula ask students to analyze or compare political organizations in different societies. A confederacy is an example of a voluntary association of peoples to support one another.

Sun Dance

An important ceremony practiced by Plains peoples to celebrate the renewal of nature.

The Blackfoot were not a single tribe but a confederacy of three tribes speaking closely related Algonquian-based dialects: the Siksika (or Blackfoot proper), the Kainah (or Bloods), and the Piegan. The three groups were split into bands, whose leaders were chosen for their bravery, wisdom, and wealth. Each group had a head chief elected by the band leaders, and all important matters were decided in councils between the band leaders and head chiefs.

Social organization

Between June and September the various Blackfoot bands came together in tribal circle camps, where they played games, feasted, boasted of their exploits, and celebrated the Sun Dance. They also hunted buffalo, and after the hunt no part of the animal was wasted: the tongues and prime cuts of meat were used in the Sun Dance feasts, and other parts of the animal were preserved for home or trading purposes.

A strong sense of tribal identity was created by the formation of men's and women's societies. Membership cut across residential groups and prevented the Blackfoot from being just a loose collection of bands. All males belonged to a warrior society, apart from effeminate males, who were known as *berdaches*. These men, who were often highly respected, dressed in women's clothes and became skilled in female crafts such as tanning and beadwork.

Organizing for war

Blackfoot warrior societies were based on a hierarchy of age and ritual. Once the oldest members of the warrior society retired, then each of the younger groups moved up one place. But as a warrior advanced, he was expected to buy the songs, privileges, and duties of the next group, and so on. Sometimes, as part of his payment, the advancing warrior had to give up his wife for a period, or if he was unmarried, borrow one from a relative.

Ritualized warfare

The Plains warfare that the warriors engaged in was also highly ritualized, with tactics based on sending small raiding parties to exact revenge or steal horses. This type of constant fighting helped unify the group against a "common" enemy—who the enemy was at the time did not matter.

Curriculum Context

A comparison of social organizations and values in different groups will help gain a deeper understanding of Native American cultures.

Blackfoot

Language:	Algonquian
Area:	Northern Plains
Reservation:	Montana and Alberta, Canada
Population:	15,000 Pre-Contact; approximately 32,000 today
Housing:	Tepees
European contact:	Trappers and hunters in the 18th century
Neighbors:	Crow, Gros Ventre, Kutenai, Plains Cree, Shoshoni
Lifestyle:	Nomadic buffalo hunters and warriors
Food:	Buffalo, deer, and fish
Crafts:	Tanning, wood, and quillwork

Although they lived on the Great Plains in the mid-1800s, many Blackfoot finally settled in Canada.

The bravest act for a Blackfoot warrior was to steal an enemy's weapons. Killing the enemy came way down the list, but even that act was ranked according to how it was done and the weapon used. Sometimes the victims' scalps (the skin on their heads) were cut off as proof of a kill, and these might be used in celebrations afterward. One of the main ways for Blackfoot warriors to acquire status within the group was by counting coup.

Ritual of daily life

Like most Plains groups, the Blackfoot's main source of food was buffalo, supplemented with moose, deer, rabbit, and gathered roots, seeds, and berries. While the men made weapons and hunted, the women did household chores and gathered wild plants.

When they moved, they folded up their tepees and carried their possessions on a *travois*, a type of sled made from two poles tied across a horse's back. Successful warriors had many wives, whom they needed to process their kill—preparing the buffalo hides was a long and difficult task—before selling it to the white traders.

This photograph, taken in 1907, shows a group of Blackfoot warriors in traditional costume.

The Sun Dance

The Sun Dance, the most important Blackfoot ritual, required the cooperation of both men and women's societies. The dancers purified themselves in a sweat lodge before putting up a sacred tree in the center of a circular brush enclosure. The full ceremony lasted eight days, during which the worshippers performed a series of rituals and prayers directed at the sun. In the ceremony worshippers used the medicine bundle, which included objects that were symbols of spiritual powers, such as a feather, stone pipe, or lock of hair.

Social divisions

The trade with white people created social divisions among the Blackfoot based on wealth in what had previously been an egalitarian society. Wealth, in the form of horses, became a symbol of bravery— since they were usually stolen from someone else. Successful warriors boasted of their prowess by giving gifts.

Blackfoot religion

Much of the Plains natives' spiritual life centered on animal powers—the strength of the buffalo, the speed of the antelope, the bravery of the eagle—and the great stars (the sun and moon), which controlled the day and night, and the seasonal cycles.

The rise and fall

In the mid-18th century, as the Blackfoot expanded their hunting and raiding territories, they became enemies with many tribes, eventually driving the Shoshoni and Kutenai into the Rockies. Their first meetings with white people were friendly; but when white trappers and hunters working for the American Fur Company started encroaching on their territory, the Blackfoot fought back. Sometimes they raided the trappers' trading posts for furs that they then sold on to the rival Hudson's Bay Company. By the 1850s, under their most famous leader, Chief Crowfoot, the Blackfoot

Curriculum Context

The study of how economic developments and interaction with white settlers affected Native American societies is included in many curricula.

The Blackfeet Nation in Montana covers some 1.5 million acres of Glacier National Park. It is home to about 7,000 Piegan Blackfeet.

Curriculum Context

Students may be required to evaluate the effects of disease, the loss of buffalo, and federal Indian policy on Native American groups. The Blackfoot suffered more from disease and the loss of their food supply than from the effects of war.

controlled a considerable territory. Preferring negotiation to conflict, Crowfoot turned down Sitting Bull's invitation to join in the wars of the Sioux and their allies against the United States. However, from the late 1860s until the 1880s, the Blackfoot were defeated not by war but by a mixture of smallpox—claiming two-thirds of their population—and the end of the buffalo herds. They were forced to sign a treaty and moved onto a reservation spanning southern Alberta and northern Montana. Today there are 32,000 Blackfoot, including several thousand who continue to live on the reservation.

Caddo

The Caddo are the direct descendants of nomadic hunters who gathered wild seeds and berries for food before they became farmers about 500 CE. Their main settlement was around the Red River Valley, where they and other friendly groups built clusters of villages. The confederacy grew until its homelands spread across parts of Arkansas, Louisiana, Oklahoma, and Texas.

The name Caddo comes from *Kadohadacho*, which means "real chiefs." One of the groups in the Caddo confederacy was the Tejas. This name was adapted to "Texas" and later applied to the state.

Hardworking and inventive

The Caddo planted large fields of corn, pumpkin, and vegetables around their villages. In summer they wore little or no clothing and worked hard in the fields. Winter, on the other hand, was usually spent making and repairing bows and arrows, clothing, and tools.

Confederacy

A league or alliance. Native American confederacies often included several united tribes or bands which formed an association to support one another.

A Caddo dancer wearing traditional dress. Dances are an important feature of Caddo social activities and ceremonies.

Curriculum Context

The curriculum may ask students to compare traditional forms of shelter in different Native American groups.

The Caddo built two types of house, one grass-thatched and the other earth-covered. The houses were grouped around an open communal space where ceremonies and meetings took place. Inside, the houses had couches that served as seats by day and beds by night. In the center of the house was a fire that was kept burning day and night. Often as many as 10 families lived in one house and farmed the land around it in common. In each household one woman was in charge of food supplies. If a house was destroyed by fire or some similar accident, other group members would help the families build a replacement.

Curriculum Context

Caddo society is an example of a chiefdom, one form of social organization among native peoples.

Tribal organization

Caddo society was organized around a great chief, or Xinesi, who controlled other chiefs or governors called Caddi. Beneath the Caddi were subchiefs named Canahas, and beneath them were Chayas, who instructed ordinary tribe members in working hard and obeying orders.

Caddo

Language:	Caddoan
Area:	Red River Valley, Louisiana; Brazos River Valley, Texas; and Arkansas
Reservation:	Oklahoma
Population:	8,000 in late 1600s; 2,549 in 1990
Housing:	Domed, grass-thatched house
European contact:	Spanish conquistador Hernando de Soto in 1541
Neighbors:	Comanche, Tonkawa, and Wichita
Lifestyle:	Villagers, farmers, and buffalo hunters
Food:	Corn and buffalo meat
Crafts:	Pottery, mats, carved wooden figures

Religious beliefs

The Caddo believed in a great spirit, Ayanat Caddi, who was the creator god. The Caddo, like many other Native American peoples, believed that everything in nature had some sort of power that could be prayed to, reasoned with, and persuaded to help them survive. One of their religious ceremonies, the Turkey Dance, is still performed today. It is an important part of the ceremony that the dance must be satisfactorily completed by the time the sun goes down.

Tribal conflicts

In the 18th century the Caddo way of life changed forever. European traders and settlers displaced whole villages, creating conflict among the Native American groups. By the end of the century the Caddo were at war with the Choctaw, who were moving into their lands. Later, however, the Caddo allied with the Choctaw against the Osage.

Sold out

In 1835 the Caddo sold their lands in Louisiana to the U.S. government for $40,000, which was paid in horses, goods, and cash annuities. They then moved to Oklahoma and Texas and later signed the Council Springs Treaty, in which they agreed to live peacefully under the protection of the U.S. government. However, by 1859 they were under attack from white Texans and were forced to leave their homes. Over a thousand Caddo men, women, and children were forced to march north in the August heat to Choctaw lands, with the Texans pursuing them.

The Caddo settled on a reservation in Oklahoma. A new tribal organization was formed, and its charter was approved by the U.S. government in 1936. However, since the 17th century their numbers have continually dropped. Among the surviving Caddo, the traditional way of life has almost disappeared.

> **Curriculum Context**
>
> Curricula often include a comparative study of religious beliefs and practices in Native American communities.

Cherokee

The Cherokee people have always been one of the largest tribal groups in America. Before the first European contact they inhabited much of the East Coast from what is now southwest Virginia to Alabama, including the entire Cumberland Basin. Today the Cherokee are primarily concentrated in eastern Oklahoma, western North Carolina, and other areas of the south.

The term Cherokee came from the Creek word *Cha-ho-kye*, which means "people who speak a different language." Since they have always been a large group, the Cherokee used different names to refer to themselves, such as *Aniyunwiya* or *Anniyaya*, which both roughly translate as "first people." Today most Cherokee prefer the term *Tsalagi* or *Tsalagihi Ayili* (Cherokee Nation).

European contact

The Cherokee had always been settled traders, and this escalated after the first European contact in 1540. Trading with the European groups, who were often at war, caused a significant shift from a spiritual leadership known as White Chiefs to a warrior leadership known as Red Chiefs. As more contact with Europeans occurred, the traditional wattle-and-daub Cherokee villages began to give way to log-cabin houses, and the people adopted European-style clothing.

By the early 1800s, the Cherokee were known to their European neighbors as one of the Five Civilized Tribes. The other four were the Chickasaw, Choctaw, Creek, and Seminole. The Cherokee had an elected central government and had developed their own free public-school systems before free schooling was available to many of their U.S. neighbors. They adopted a constitutional-style government and established a legal system that included a "supreme court."

Wattle-and-daub

A building material traditionally used for making walls and consisting of an interwoven lattice of wooden sticks, covered with a material such as clay.

Curriculum Context

Students can use diverse forms of tribal organization and government to explore the differences and similarities between native cultures.

This lithograph shows Sequoyah, inventor of the Cherokee alphabet. The alphabet consists of 86 characters used to represent specific sounds.

In 1821 the Cherokee leader Sequoyah published a unique alphabet, the only widespread written Native American language. Shortly afterward a printing press was adapted to the new alphabet, and within months most of the Cherokee became literate in both the Cherokee language (which is related to the Iroquois languages) and English. By 1830 the Cherokee literacy rate was higher than that of the United States in the year 2000. This was helped by the publication of the *Cherokee Phoenix*, a newspaper written in both English and Cherokee, first printed in 1828.

Indian Removal Act and the Trail of Tears

Inevitable conflict with the U.S. government started when gold was discovered on Cherokee territory. Gold prospectors pressured Congress to forcibly remove all Native American people east of the Mississippi River. In 1830 the Indian Removal Act stripped the Cherokee and other Native Americans of their property and forcibly marched them from their homelands in the southern United States to the new so-called Indian Territory in Oklahoma.

Indian Removal Act

A federal law signed by President Andrew Jackson in 1830 authorizing the removal of Native Americans from their lands in the east and their resettlement in the west.

On this march, which has become known as the Trail of Tears, more than one-quarter of the people died. The government reneged on its promise to leave ownership of ancestral lands with the Cherokee and instead took control of the land and sold it to speculators.

The Cherokee today

Today there are three federally recognized Cherokee groups. First is the United Keetoowah Band of Oklahoma (UKB), with 10,000 members and less than 50 acres of tribally owned land. They follow a traditional Cherokee lifestyle. Second is the Eastern Band of Cherokee of North Carolina, descendants of about 1,000 Cherokee who refused to relocate to Oklahoma and remained hidden in the remote areas of the Great Smoky Mountains. Today tourism comprises most of their economy. The third and largest group is the Cherokee Nation of Oklahoma, numbering more than 200,000 enrolled members. The Cherokee Nation takes a lead in issues such as education reform, housing, vocational training, and health care. The government leadership is organized around a primary chief who presides over the various local governments.

Today there is a resurgence of traditional skills and culture, with new interest in the Cherokee language, dances such as the stomp, and traditional crafts such as split-oak basket making, pottery, and wood carving. Although conditions continue to improve for the federally recognized Cherokee groups, the majority of the Cherokee people are "nonrecognized" by the U.S. government. More than 220 communities and several hundreds of thousands of people in Oklahoma and the southern states consider themselves Cherokee but are not enrolled in any Cherokee sovereign nation.

Cheyenne

The Cheyenne occupied the western Plains during the 19th century. Their name came from their neighbors the Sioux, who called them *Shahiyena* (meaning "speakers of an unintelligible language"). Originally a farming tribe from Minnesota, the Cheyenne were driven out by the Sioux and Ojibway in the late 17th century.

The Cheyenne migrated westward along what is now known as the Cheyenne River, settling in North Dakota. About 1770 the Ojibway destroyed their settlements again, forcing them to move into the Black Hills of South Dakota, where they changed almost overnight from farmers to buffalo hunters.

The new tribe of the Plains

After acquiring horses, the Cheyenne became one of the dominant tribes of the western Plains, with a reputation as fierce warriors. This was one of many rapid changes in their culture that occurred after the move from a farming to a nomadic lifestyle—they also acquired the tepee, the Sun Dance, and social divisions based on wealth in horses.

> ### Curriculum Context
>
> The changes that took place in Cheyenne culture and way of life after they moved to the Plains are good examples of how native peoples adjusted their lifestyles to their natural environment.

This drawing by the Cheyenne artist Making Medicine was created in 1875. It shows a group of Cheyenne on a bear hunt.

Tribal organization

Of all the Plains peoples, the Cheyenne had the most organized tribal government. The Cheyenne were made up of 10 separate bands. These bands were in fact extended households passed on through the wife or mother. Men marrying into a different band moved to the lodges of their wife's relatives, although they retained strong links with their own blood relatives as well. The bands were essentially self-sufficient and were under the leadership of a band chief. Throughout most of the year they camped independently of other bands.

The Cheyenne tribe was governed by a council of 44 men who would meet during the summer circle camp, when all the bands came together. Always forming the same layout, each band took up its designated position within the campground. The previous year's council would elect four council members from each of the ten bands. They would also choose four head chiefs regardless of band affiliation.

It was also during the annual tribal camp that major renewal ceremonies were performed under the ritual control of a highly respected shaman (medicine man) known as the "Keeper of the Sacred Medicine Arrows."

Warrior societies

In addition to their band and tribal organization, the Cheyenne had several warrior societies. The members of these societies were usually men, although there were some honorary female warriors. Membership in a warrior society, unlike a tribal band, was usually inherited through the father. The two most famous and feared of the warrior societies were the Contraries and the Dog Soldiers. Only the bravest warriors could belong to the Contraries, who were given their name because nearly all of their daily actions were contradictory. For example, they said "no" when they meant "yes" and when they were summoned they went away. The Dog Soldiers had a reputation for ferocity because of their resolve to "no-flight." This was a pledge never to retreat from battle but to continue fighting until they either won or were killed.

The spirit world

The Cheyenne, like other Plains peoples, had a rich ceremonial life and an interest in the stars. An aspect they took seriously was the Vision Quest. It was an individual ritual in which young men pursued their vision through isolation, fasting, exposure to the sun, and self-torture—activities that were known to provoke hallucinations—and begged the spirits to take pity on their suffering. Not everyone was successful, but it was believed that if a spirit did take pity on a young warrior, it gave him supernatural guidance that would support him for the rest of his life.

The Cheyenne also adapted the Sun Dance, an annual group ceremony of the Plains tribes. Their version

Vision Quest

A rite of passage in many Native American groups, in which young individuals go alone to an isolated place to seek protection from the spirits.

Cheyenne

Language:	Algonquian
Area:	Western Plains
Reservation:	Oklahoma and Montana
Population:	3,500 Pre-Contact; approximately 11,000 today
Housing:	Tepee
European contact:	Settlers in the 1840s
Neighbors:	Crow, Sioux, and Arapaho
Lifestyle:	Nomadic buffalo hunters and warriors
Food:	Buffalo and antelope
Crafts:	Tanning, quillwork, and headdresses

After the mid-1800s the Cheyenne were split in two.

This photograph, taken in 1910, shows a Cheyenne Sun Dance lodge. The annual Sun Dance ceremony celebrated continuity between life and death and renewal in nature. It lasted from four to eight days and the building of the lodge was an important symbolic part of the ritual.

included trials of deprivation, since they believed that suffering would call up supernatural aid.

Wars with the United States

Up until the mid-1850s the Cheyenne had been peaceful toward settlers. Then, in 1851 the Fort Laramie Treaty imposed by the United States separated the northern Cheyenne living on the North Platte from the southern Cheyenne on the Upper Arkansas River. This group was allied closely with the Arapaho.

In 1861 the U.S. government persuaded the Cheyenne to move to a small reservation in Colorado, but there were not enough animals to provide sufficient food so some of the braves started cattle rustling. The governor of Colorado, John Evans, meanwhile, wanted to open up the new Cheyenne territory to gold prospectors. The Cheyenne refused to sell their hunting grounds to the state, so Evans called on a group of Colorado militia led by Colonel John M. Chivington to wage a bloody campaign against them. When some of his officers objected, the colonel is reported to have said: "Damn any man who sympathizes with Indians. I have come to kill Indians and believe it's right and honorable to use any means under God's heaven to kill Indians."

Sand Creek Massacre

In November 1864 Chivington's soldiers attacked a group of unarmed Cheyenne and Arapaho men, women, and children at Sand Creek. Of the 400 Native Americans who were killed and mutilated there, over half were women and children. When news of the massacre reached the other Cheyenne, they went on the warpath and continued to harass the U.S. Army for over a decade.

Relocation to Oklahoma

In 1876 the Cheyenne joined with their Sioux allies for their greatest victory over the United States. Together they defeated Lieutenant Colonel George Custer and his troops at the Battle of Little Bighorn. But thecelebrations among the Plains peoples did not last long. Within a year of Little Bighorn, after a series of defeats, the Cheyenne and their allies surrendered and were forced by the government to relocate to Oklahoma. Today there are an estimated 11,000 Cheyenne, many of whom still live on reservations in Oklahoma and Montana.

Comanche

The Shoshonean-speaking Comanche were a nomadic tribe of the Plains who hunted buffalo. In the 18th century they occupied an area stretching from the Platte River in Nebraska to the Mexican border. The Comanche's culture and economy were typical of southern Plains tribes. Their warriors were renowned for outstanding acts of bravery and excellent horsemanship.

Band

A simple form of human society consisting of an extended kin or family group. Bands are smaller than tribes and have fewer social institutions.

The Comanche were divided into bands. The movements of these bands were dictated by the movements of the buffalo on which the Comanche depended for food and clothing. The meaning of band names, such as Making Bags While Moving, Those Who Move Often, and Wanderers, reflects the lifestyle of tribal migration typical of the Comanche.

Horse raiders

Wishing to secure new hunting grounds, the Comanche appeared in New Mexico in 1705 on a peace mission to the Caddo tribe. On leaving, they stole some horses, and this marked their arrival as the "greatest horse raiders of them all." Throughout the 1700s raiding activities brought them into conflict with the Apache and the Spanish. Although a Comanche–Spanish treaty in 1786 brought a temporary halt to excursions south of the U.S.–Mexico border, with Spanish encouragement the Comanche increased their raids on the Apache.

Equestrian skills

The Comanche were among the first Plains peoples to acquire horses, most of which were obtained by raiding Spanish and Mexican settlements. They became famous for skills in roping and training mustangs that roamed wild in the region. Much of the average male Comanche's time was spent on horseback. In the 1830s artist George Catlin said Comanche men seemed awkward when walking but on horseback they became the most elegant and skillful equestrian warriors in North America.

Allies and enemies

Comanche relations with the Pueblo peoples of the Southwest were good, with trading at Taos in New Mexico. Friendly contacts were also maintained with the Cheyenne, Kiowa, and Arapaho, although in the 1830s a Comanche–Kiowa alliance briefly turned against the southern Cheyenne and Arapaho living along the Arkansas River and defeated them. By the 1840s friendly relations between the Cheyenne and Comanche had been restored.

Both the Comanche and Kiowa tribes remained at peace with the United States, although the Comanche did not extend this privilege to citizens of Texas—who in 1848 declared war on the Comanche against U.S. wishes—and continued to consider Texans and Mexicans as their sworn enemies.

Pueblo peoples
Native American village-dwelling peoples of the Southwest, including modern-day New Mexico and Arizona.

Comanche

Language:	Shoshonean
Area:	Southern Plains
Reservation:	Oklahoma
Population:	7,000 Pre-Contact; approximately 6,250 today
Housing:	Tepee
European contact:	Spanish in the 17th century
Neighbors:	Kiowa, Wichita, and Apache
Lifestyle:	Nomads and warriors
Food:	Buffalo and other game, roots, and berries
Crafts:	Skinwork and beadwork

The Comanche were among the most skilled riders of the Plains.

A set of three separate treaties signed in 1867 at Medicine Lodge Creek, Kansas, between the U.S. government and the Kiowa, Comanche, Plains Apache, Southern Cheyenne, and Arapaho. The treaties involved the surrender of tribal homelands in exchange for reservations in the Indian Territory.

Texan pressure finally brought about a further treaty, the Medicine Lodge Treaty of 1867, under which the Comanche were to be removed to the Indian Territory, in present-day Oklahoma. Many Comanche refused to go, claiming that they had only fought against Texans and had remained friendly to their American allies. The aging chief Ten Bears, of the Yamparika (Root-eaters) band, made an impassioned speech to the treaty commissioners against the removal, but his plea was unsuccessful.

Many members of the Comanche, Kiowa, and Cheyenne tribes did not want to be removed and joined forces under Quanah Parker, the leader of the Kwahadi (Antelopes) and the son of a Nokoni (Wanderer) chief and an adopted white woman.

This photograph, taken in 1927, shows Esipermi, a member of the Comanche.

War and defeat

Under Quanah Parker a Comanche alliance waged war on both the U.S. forces deployed against them and commercial buffalo hunters who entered tribal territories in increasing numbers throughout the 1870s. However, Comanche resistance was a last and futile attempt to save the remaining southern buffalo herds. Increased military pressure saw the destruction of Comanche, Kiowa, and southern Cheyenne camps, demoralizing the groups and leaving them with poor shelter, clothing, horses, weapons, and ammunition. In 1875 a final violent confrontation at Llano Estacado (the Staked Plains of western Texas and southeastern New Mexico) between the poorly equipped Comanche–Kiowa and the troops of General Nelson Miles forced the Comanche to abandon their homelands. After this defeat the Comanche became virtual prisoners on reservations in Oklahoma.

Comanche crafts

Enforced confinement resulted in the loss of many Comanche crafts from the pre-reservation period. One distinctive craft object was a high moccasin with a rawhide sole and buckskin upper. Women's moccasins, like those of the Arapaho and Apache, were knee-high and could be turned down to resemble a cuffed boot. Another lost craft from the period before contact with Europeans created a Pan-Indian Plains style was the art of delicate beadwork, including a form of bead netting used to trim dresses.

Today members of the Comanche tribe, the remnant of a once proud culture, are trying to revive early crafts and skills for commercial gain. As beadworkers the Comanche craftspeople make some of the finest, most carefully worked craft objects available to the tourist market.

Cree

The Cree are one of the largest and most important tribes of Canada. Their traditional homelands are the regions of Saskatchewan and Manitoba. These are Subarctic regions, which have long, cold winters and short summers. The Cree were the southernmost group of the major Native American Subarctic tribes, and over the centuries they developed great skill in surviving the cold climate.

When Europeans first encountered the Cree in the 17th century, bands of the group were spread over a large part of the continent. The Cree hunted in an area stretching from the Ottawa River in present-day Quebec to the Saskatchewan River of western Canada.

Forest people

Originally, the Cree were a forest people. They lived in cone-shaped tents covered with birchbark and moved around most of the year. They hunted all sorts of animals, including caribou, moose, bear, deer, beaver, and rabbit. The Cree built canoes out of birchbark to carry them along the great rivers and lakes of the area. In winter they wore snowshoes.

Curriculum Context

Students learning about pre-Columbian societies might be asked to describe how geography and climate influenced the lifestyles of Native American groups.

In this way the Cree were able to survive the long, cold winters, but there were often times when they could find nothing to eat. At such times the tribe relied on their shamans (medicine men) to locate food sources.

The Cree lifestyle

The Cree wore warm clothes made from the hides of animals, especially the caribou. They used quills and feathers to decorate their clothes.

When the Cree began to trade with European settlers in the 17th century, they also started to use precious metals and stones to decorate their clothes and tools.

Allies and enemies

The Cree were part of the Algonquian-speaking group of Native Americans. Their principal allies were the Assiniboine, a tribe that came from western Saskatchewan, Canada. The Cree were frequently at war with neighboring groups, and their traditional enemies were the Blackfoot and the Sioux.

In times of war the different bands of Cree formed larger groups to attack their enemies. Together with the Assiniboine, the Cree were responsible for forcing the Blackfoot from western Saskatchewan.

Cree bands

There were several different bands of the Cree in Canada. The Swampy Cree lived in the wet north country near Hudson Bay, while the Western Wood Cree lived in the forests north of Lake Winnipeg. The Eastern Wood Cree lived in the present-day province of Quebec.

This engraving shows an early Cree encampmen Originally the Cr were nomadic for dwellers who live in cone-shaped tents and moved from one place to another in search of animals to hunt.

The Plains Cree were a group who moved southward out of the forests and onto the Great Plains. Here they hunted buffalo along with other native peoples, such as the Blackfoot.

In due course some of the Plains Cree chose to abandon living in their traditional bark-covered tents. Instead, they began to live in tepees made of animal skin as other Plains Native Americans did.

Trading tribe

The Cree were geographically well placed to trade with other Native American peoples such as the Chipewan to the north and the Ojibway to the south.

During the 17th century the Cree were among the first Native American peoples to trade with the French and the English. Their skill in trapping animals impressed the Europeans, who relied on them as hunters and scouts in the forests and swamps of the area.

Cree

Language:	Algonquian
Area:	Subarctic
Reservation:	Eastern Canada and Montana
Population:	25,000 Pre-Contact; approximately 80,000 today
Housing:	Wigwams and bark and brush shelters
European contact:	French and English traders, early 1800s
Neighbors:	Inuit, Blackfoot, Sioux, and Ojibway
Lifestyle:	Hunting and gathering
Food:	Caribou, small game, fish, roots, and berries
Crafts:	Barkwork and beadwork

The Cree are one of the largest and most important tribes in Canada.

Crow

The Crow originally came from the plains and prairies of Knife River, North Dakota, and belong to the Siouan-speaking family. Crow legends tell us that the group was once allied with the Hidatsa, but because of a dispute over buffalo they migrated west to the Yellowstone River in Montana during the late 17th century or early 18th century.

The Crow who settled to the north were called Mountain Crow, and those who went south became the River Crow. The Hidatsa were a settled people who lived in villages and grew crops. When the Crow split from them, they became nomadic, moving around in search of game to hunt. They adopted the way of life of the Plains Native Americans who lived in portable

Nomadic

Having no permanent home and moving from one place to another according to the seasons in search of hunting grounds, water, and grazing land.

A member of the Mountain Crow, photographed in 1908, with bow and arrow and traditional feather headdress. The Crow are said to have owned more horses per person than any other Plains people.

tepees made of hide, hunting buffalo and other game. During the 18th century the Crow started riding horses, which helped them when they hunted.

Family life
The Crow had a highly developed social structure in which the upbringing of children was very important. Crow fathers held feasts in their children's honor, praising them and foretelling their future success in life. Fathers also spent a lot of time teaching their sons hunting skills, such as how to shoot game using a bow and arrows. The mothers taught their daughters the domestic skills they would need when they grew up, such as how to prepare food and make clothes.

Religious beliefs
The Crow also had a complex set of religious beliefs. When a member of the group died, he or she would be put on a platform high in a tree. In this way the body would be kept away from animals on the ground.

Curriculum Context

A comparative study of burial rituals in different groups will help students understand the diverse religious beliefs of Native American peoples.

Crow

The Crow live near the Yellowstone and Bighorn rivers, Montana.

Language:	Siouan
Area:	Yellowstone and Bighorn rivers, Montana
Reservation:	Montana
Population:	4,000 Pre-Contact; approximately 8,000 today
Housing:	Tepee
European contact:	French, English, and Americans in the 1700s
Neighbors:	Missouri River tribes, Blackfoot, and Sioux
Lifestyle:	Nomads and warriors
Food:	Buffalo and other game, roots, and berries
Crafts:	Skinwork and beadwork

Horse raiders

During the 19th century the great herds of buffalo that had once roamed the Plains, providing food, shelter, and clothing for many groups of native peoples, began to die out. They had been overhunted by Native Americans and by Europeans, both of whom had horses and guns. However, the Crow did not rely just on hunting for their survival. Horse raiding and trading were also very important. In 1821 European traders held a meeting along the Arkansas River with Cheyenne, Arapaho, Comanche, and Kiowa Native Americans. They posted many guards around their camp, but every night Crow warriors would steal in and escape with their horses. The Crow became well known for their fast, stealthy way of rustling horses.

Like other Plains peoples, the Crow celebrated the annual Sun Dance. They also practiced the Vision Quest, a ritual in which they tried to foresee the future for children who were becoming adults. In this ritual they used tobacco, the only crop they grew. In 1904 the U.S. government banned the Sun Dance along with all other Native American ceremonies. Its aim was to try to prevent the native peoples from forming strong social, cultural, and religious bonds with each other. The government feared that a unified group of Native American peoples would resist its program of resettlement on the reservations, which in many cases had taken land away from the tribes. The Sun Dance was revived in a new form after 1941.

Allies and enemies

In the 19th century the Crow also became known for siding with the U.S. Army against other Native American groups, especially their traditional enemies the Sioux. Many of the Crow became scouts for the U.S. Army.

One Crow member, nicknamed Curley, was a scout for the Seventh Cavalry detachment led by Lieutenant Colonel George Custer at the Battle of Little Bighorn. This famous battle took place in June 1876 and was remembered in history as the day the Native Americans defeated the U.S. Army. Custer and more than 200 of his troops were killed. Curley was one of the few survivors of the battle on the army's side. Today there is a Custer Battleground National Monument on the Crow reservation in Montana, and every year there is a reenactment of the famous battle.

The Crow chiefs sided with the U.S. Army against other Native American groups for two main reasons: first, as a way of defeating their traditional Native American enemies; and second, to gain special treatment from the U.S. government once the fighting was finished. However, the plan failed. The Crow were treated in exactly the same way as other native peoples, and were not granted any favors because of their help.

Crow reservation

As the 19th century progressed, the building of forts and railroads brought more settlers into the Crow's homelands, and soon the group's traditional way of life came to an end. The Fort Laramie Treaty in 1851 granted the Crow nearly 40 million acres (16 million ha) in southern Montana, northern Wyoming, and western South Dakota. A second Fort Laramie treaty signed in 1868 gave the Crow a reservation in southeastern Montana. However, during the 1880s settlers built forts, and railroads were established on the Crow's land. By 1883 the buffalo herds had disappeared, and by 1888 the Crow had been forced to give up most of its former lands.

During the 20th century, oil was discovered on the Crow reservation, which provided some much-needed income for the group. By 1990 more than 8,000 people in the United States claimed that they had Crow ancestry.

Curriculum Context

The curriculum may ask students to examine how Native American societies changed as a result of the gradual dispossession of their land and U.S. territorial expansion.

Delaware

In 1610 Captain Samuel Argall was exploring the coast north of Jamestown when he discovered a bay which he named in honor of Sir Thomas West, 12th Baron De La Warre and governor of Virginia. Governor West returned to England, but the name stuck, and English colonists began to use the word Delaware to mean the bay, the river, and the people who lived there.

The *Grandfathers*

Delaware is not actually a Native American name. The Delaware people call themselves *Lenni Lenape*, meaning "men of our nation," "original people," or "true men." The Algonquian-speaking peoples call the Lenape "Grandfathers," a term of respect reflecting their belief that the Lenape were the original tribe of all the Algonquian-speaking peoples.

Among the Algonquian-speaking peoples, the Lenape had the authority to settle disputes between rival groups. When the French first discovered the Lenape, they called them *loup*, or wolf, because of their bravery.

Tribal groups

The Lenape had lived in the Delaware River valley for hundreds of years before the Europeans encountered them. They were made up of three groups that spoke different dialects: the Munsee, or "people of the stony country"; the Unami, or "people down the river"; and the Unalactigo, or "people near the ocean."

Curriculum Context

Many curricula ask students to study the diversity in languages in Native American societies.

Tribal society

The Lenape were divided into clans according to the ancestry of the mother. There were three clans: the Turtle, the Wolf, and the Turkey. Each clan had a leader, or *swachem*, who inherited the position by birth. However, the position had to be confirmed by a vote from the people. The head of the Delaware Wolf clan

Clan

A social unit consisting of a number of households or families with a common ancestor.

in 1775 was called Konieschquanoheel, meaning "maker of daylight." His nickname, however, was Hopocan, meaning "tobacco pipe," and he thus became known as Captain Pipe.

The Lenape lifestyle

The Lenape were a settled people who farmed squash, beans, sweet potatoes, and tobacco. Farming was solely the women's responsibility, while the men did the hunting and fishing using dugout canoes.

The Lenape men removed all their facial hair. The women colored their faces with red ocher. The older men wore their hair greased to stand up high. Today this style is often known as a "Mohican." Many Woodland and Prairie tribes adopted it.

Lenape clothing was made from deerskin, decorated with beads, porcupine quills, and feathers. The Lenape

Delaware

Colonists used the word "Delaware" for a bay, a river, and a people.

Language:	Algonquian
Area:	Atlantic seaboard; Delaware River Valley
Reservation:	Oklahoma, Wisconsin, and Ontario
Population:	12,000 Pre-Contact; approximately 3,000 today
Housing:	Domed wigwams and longhouses
European contact:	Verrazano 1524; Dutch and Swedish fur traders in 1600s; British settlers later
Neighbors:	Wappinger and Susquehannock
Lifestyle:	Hunting; farming corn, beans, and squash
Food:	Game, corn, beans, and squash
Crafts:	Carving and skinwork

also used copper, which they acquired via trade with native groups from the western Great Lakes.

The spirit world

There were two types of shaman (medicine man) in the Lenape group: dream interpreters and healers. The Lenape saw dreams as signs which needed to be carefully interpreted.

The Lenape also believed in evil spirits and would often refuse to reveal their real names in case the spirits should hear them.

Contact with Europeans

The Lenape first encountered Europeans in 1524, when Giovanni da Verrazano, an Italian navigator, entered New York Harbor through the strait now named after him. He anchored off Staten Island and met the Lenape there.

The Lenape were friendly and curious toward the European newcomers, but Verrazano tried to kidnap some of them before he left. Thereafter, the Lenape treated the Europeans with distrust.

Curriculum Context

Students learning about the relationships between Native American groups and white settlers could focus on the reasons for the Lenape's changing attitudes.

Tribal conflicts

As the Dutch fur trade grew, the Lenape's peaceful life came to an end. There was war among the Native American tribes, especially between the Lenape and the Susquehannock over hunting territory. By 1640 the Lenape had been defeated, and all the beaver had been hunted from the area.

Losing homelands

In 1682 the Lenape sold some of their land to William Penn, a Quaker colonist who treated the group with respect and honesty. However, Penn's descendants were less fair and forced many of the Lenape out of their homelands.

Curriculum Context

Students may be asked to explore treaties made between the U.S. government and Native American groups and assess the long-term outcomes of these treaties.

Treaty with the United States

In 1778 the Lenape (now known as the Delaware) signed the first treaty made between a Native American group and the United States. The treaty granted the Lenape people representation in Congress. By 1794, however, the Lenape were at war with the United States and were defeated at the Battle of Fallen Timbers in Ohio. Over the following century the group's numbers were depleted by war and disease. The Lenape were cheated out of their lands and were repeatedly moved to different reservations by successive U.S. governments.

This detail of a painting created by Benjamin West in 1771, depicts William Penn negotiating with the Lenape.

Five Civilized Tribes

The Five Civilized Tribes—the Cherokee, Chickasaw, Choctaw, Creek, and Seminole—were so-called by European settlers because their lives were organized in a way that reminded the colonists of their own. They were mostly settled peoples who lived in villages and towns, grew crops such as corn, and had strong social structures, often with elected leaders.

Such ways of life were centuries old, but white settlers tended to assume that the groups had learned them from Europeans who had visited the area earlier, and the whites ignored those aspects of tribal culture that had little in common with European ways.

Tribal homelands

The Five Civilized Tribes were based in the Southeast. The Cherokee originated in the north, near the Great Lakes, but by the time they first encountered Europeans in the mid-16th century, they were settled in the southern Appalachians, particularly the Carolinas. The Choctaw's homelands were in south and central Mississippi, while the closely related Chickasaw—the two may well once have been one tribe—were centered in northern Alabama and Mississippi, and the Seminole were based in Florida.

The Creek were a loose confederacy of peoples known by their Algonquian neighbors as the Muskogee, "the People of the Creeks." The confederacy, which dated from before the first European contact, included people from some 30 towns in the area.

Some tribes intermarried with the Muskogee, while others stayed as ethnic minorities within the two main Creek territories. The Upper Creek lived in Alabama and the Lower Creek in eastern Georgia and along the Atlantic coast.

Curriculum Context

A comparision of the lifestyle and culture of the Five Civilized Tribes before and after European contact will help students understand the extent of European influence on these groups.

Although there were differences among the Five Civilized Tribes, there also were striking similarities. They were all organized into clans and towns. However, towns could be scattered and informal, as with the Chickasaw, or structured around a central square, as with the Creek. Councils of elders—both men and women were involved—looked after the groups' affairs. In the case of the Creek and Cherokee, towns and councils were either red or white; red towns were concerned with waging war, and white ones with more peaceful pursuits.

Curriculum Context

Students learning about gender roles in different societies might choose to focus on the involvement of women in the government of the Five Civilized Tribes.

Growing crops

In addition to hunting and gathering, all the five groups lived by growing crops such as corn, beans, squash, and sunflowers, as well as tobacco for use in ceremonies. In the 18th and early 19th centuries many began to produce crops for cash. Some individuals became rich, running fairly large plantations.

Plantation

An estate or farm on which crops such as tobacco are cultivated.

All the five groups kept slaves; African Americans and members of other tribes were put to work in the fields alongside the women. Unlike the white plantation owners who were to follow, the Cherokee often absorbed slaves into the families and clans that owned them.

Games and ceremonies

Although tribes and clans did go to war with each other, some of the tensions between them were settled by playing games, including a form of lacrosse. Many of these games had a ritual significance.

Lacrosse was played at a midsummer festival that celebrated the corn harvest. The festival was known as the Green Corn Ceremony or the Busk. After several days of feasting, fasting, dancing, and games, the festival ended with a communal bath and a speech from the chief.

The Busk was regarded as a new beginning. Afterward all the remnants of the feast were burned, and a fire kindled for the coming year. All as yet unpunished crimes—except for murder—were forgiven.

Taking sides

The first Europeans to encounter the Five Civilized Tribes were the Spanish in the late 1530s. In the 17th century the tribes came under French influence. The Choctaw often allied themselves with the French and fought with them against the Natchez in the Natchez Rebellion of 1729. (The Five Civilized Tribes never fought the United States.) The Cherokee, on the other hand, supported the British in the American

LEDAGIE.
A CREEK CHIEF.

This lithograph, created in 1843, shows Ledagie, a Creek chief. He is wearing a traditional Creek plumed headdress.

In the late 1830s the United States forced the Five Civilized Tribes to move from their homelands in the Southeast to the Indian Territory hundreds of miles to the west. Some escaped the move, and today the tribes remain split between east and west.

Revolution to protect their homelands, and other tribes joined in raids on frontier towns.

By the fall of 1776, however, all of the British-allied Native Americans in the South had been defeated by the Revolutionary militia and were forced to give up much of their territory as a result.

After the war the Cherokee began to be assimilated by white settlers, and intermarriage became common. The Cherokee adopted many European ways. In the 1820s a Cherokee man called Sequoyah developed a written

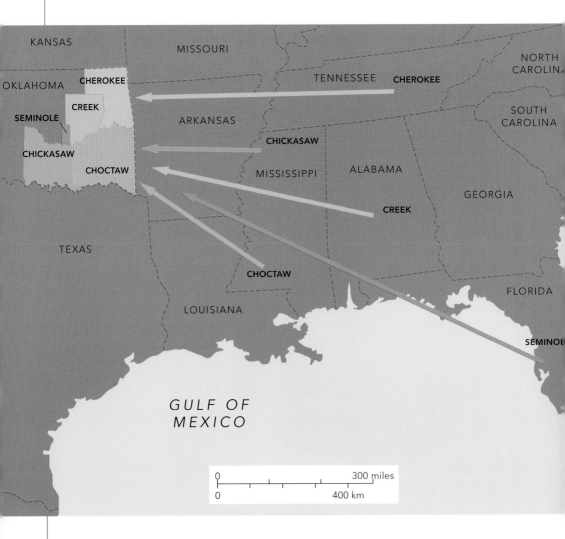

form of their language. Soon the tribe became literate, and a newspaper, *Cherokee Phoenix*, began publication at the end of the decade.

Other groups remained hostile toward the United States. In the War of 1812, some Creek towns supported the British. Soon after, a fight between two Creek factions spilled over into a massacre of frontiersmen at Fort Mims, Florida. General Andrew Jackson led a force of militia and Cherokee to victory over the Creek in 1814.

New lands

In the decade following the Indian Removal Act of 1830, which became law while Andrew Jackson was U.S. president, most of the Five Tribes were forced to relocate to the Indian Territory. Only pockets remained in North Carolina and Alabama.

Once settled in the Indian Territory, the groups were granted a form of self-government based on the U.S. model. This lasted until the Civil War of 1861–1865, when most groups supported the Confederacy. After the war they lost land and what little independence they had left.

In the late 19th century, as the Indian Territory prepared for statehood, the tribal governments were dissolved. The tribal lands were allotted to white homesteaders, but freed slaves and Native Americans were able to stake claims too. However, when the Indian Territory finally became a state (Oklahoma) in 1907, the Five Civilized Tribes lost most of their remaining territory.

Curriculum Context

Students might be asked to study federal Indian policy after the Civil War and evaluate its legacy and effects on tribal identity and land ownership.

Huron

In the late 16th century the Huron, an Iroquoian-speaking confederation of five tribes, lived in an area of central Ontario, Canada. The area, called Huronia by the French, stretches from the south part of Georgian Bay to Lake Simcoe. During the 1700s most of the Huron were driven south and west by their enemies, members of the Iroquois League.

A small group of Huron managed to remain in Ontario and Quebec. Those who were forced to move first traveled to Michigan and Ohio before settling in Kansas and later Oklahoma.

Farmers and traders

In Ontario, before the Iroquois forced them out of the region, the Huron had established a sophisticated cultural and communal life. They had built large villages and towns that were sometimes protected with a palisade (a high fence made of sharpened wooden stakes). Huron people lived in longhouses.

The Huron were mainly farmers who cleared land in order to grow their crops, which included corn, beans, squash, and sunflowers. They also hunted, fished, and gathered berries, nuts, and seeds from the forest. Women planted, cared for, and harvested the crops and also did some fishing, while the men cleared the land and hunted. When the soil became infertile or other conditions for growing crops and finding additional food became less favorable, the Huron would move to a new site where they would establish another village.

Social organization

Women were extremely important and revered in Huron tribal society. They selected all the political leaders and were influential in all decisions about clan membership,

Longhouse

A communal house shared by several families. Longhouses measured up to 200 feet (60 m) in length and were built of post frames covered in bark.

Curriculum Context

Students learning about the status of women in different cultures could focus on the important role women had in Huron society.

which was passed down through the mother's family. The clan was the basic social unit of a Huron tribal village and was governed by a clan chief. All the clan chiefs of a tribal village formed a council that was headed by a village chief, who was elected by the whole village. A number of tribal villages made up a band, which had a council consisting of all the village chiefs. Together the bands made up the Huron confederation of five tribes.

War and disease

The coming of the Europeans into what is now Canada had a devastating effect on the Huron. This took two forms: disease and war. Prior to 1630 the Huron population was about 20,000 to 30,000. Contact with Europeans led to several smallpox epidemics in the

Huron

Language:	Iroquoian
Area:	Northeast
Territory:	Quebec and Ontario in Canada; Kansas and Oklahoma in the United States
Population:	20,000–30,000 in 1615; approximately 6,500 today
Housing:	Communal bark-covered longhouses
European contact:	French fur traders and settlers, Jesuit missionaries
Neighbors:	Iroquois, Ottawa, Ojibway, and Algonquian
Lifestyle:	Agriculture supplemented by fishing, hunting, and gathering
Food:	Fish, meat, corn, beans, squash, fruit, nuts, and seeds
Arts:	Pottery

The Huron, an Iroquoian-speaking tribe, lived in the Northeast. During the first half of the 17th century they were the link between European fur traders and the native peoples that provided animal fur.

1630s, reducing the population to about 9,000. The effects of war were just as harmful as the effects of disease.

The fur trade

The Huron were well placed between the French settlements and the tribal groups to the north and west of the Great Lakes who could supply animal fur pelts. With the establishment of the French fur trade the Huron were able to act as middlemen between the French, who wanted the furs, and their neighbors, who provided them.

Curriculum Context

The conflicts between the Iroquois and Huron over trade routes are a good example of how economic developments affected Native American groups.

In the early 1700s Iroquois groups, such as the Mohawk, decided that they wanted a larger stake in the fur trade. As a result, they waged a series of wars on the Huron in order to take over their trade routes. Many Huron were killed or driven out of the region, eventually settling in the United States. Some joined neighboring groups, while others were absorbed into the Iroquois. A small number, some 300, established a settlement in Quebec under French protection.

The Huron today

Apart from the Huron living at Jeune Lorette, the only remaining descendants of the Huron are the Wyandots (or Wyandottes). Today some of these people live near Sandwich, Ontario, while others reside in Kansas and on a reservation in Wyandotte, Oklahoma.

Iroquois

The Iroquois are a group of peoples: the Mohawk, Oneida, Onondaga, Cayuga, and Seneca. In 1570 these groups joined together to form an alliance known as the Five Nations, or the Iroquois League. Later, the Tuscarora joined the league. For many years the Iroquois League was the largest and most powerful group of Native Americans in Northeast America.

The name Iroquois means "real adders" in the Algonquian language. The Algonquian people gave the tribes this name because they were so fierce in battle. Yet although the Iroquois were famous for their bravery as warriors, they also became known as statesmen and peacemakers. They called themselves *Hodenausee*, or "people of the longhouse," and developed a social and political structure based on a society in which groups of families lived peacefully together, all under one roof.

Curriculum Context

A study of the social and political structure of the Iroquois will help students understand the connections and similarities between different Native American groups.

Way of life

The Iroquois homelands were in the middle of Algonquian territory, along the valleys, lakes, and rivers of what is now upper New York State. There they built rectangular homes, often up to 200 feet (60 m) long, known as longhouses. In winter as many as a dozen

This photograph shows the inside of a reconstructed 15th-century Iroquoian ceremonial longhouse at Crawford Lake, Ontario.

Curriculum Context

The various forms of shelter that Native Americans constructed are important in understanding the lifestyles and cultures of different groups.

families lived in one house. Along the walls of each house were raised platforms that were used as seats in the day and as beds at night. There were movable holes in the roof of the longhouse that allowed fires to be lit inside and smoke to escape.

The Iroquois hunted, fished, and gathered nuts and berries. They were also great farmers, growing corn, beans, and squash. They called these three staples of their diet "the Three Sisters of the Iroquois," and they had special ceremonies to help the plants grow.

For traveling they used canoes made of elm or spruce bark. These were heavier than the birchbark canoes used by the Algonquians, but they could also be used as ladders or shields. The Iroquois men were responsible for hunting food and protecting the families, while the women, who owned the houses, cared for the children, gathered wild foods, did the cooking, and made clothing and baskets.

Iroquois

The Iroquois League was a powerful force until the early 19th century.

Language:	Iroquoian
Area:	Woodland region
Reservation:	New York State
Population:	5,500 in 17th century; approximately 50,000 today
Housing:	Longhouse
European contact:	Settlers in the 17th century
Neighbors:	Wyandot, Delaware, and Shawnee
Lifestyle:	Settled hunters and farmers
Food:	Corn, beans, and squash
Crafts:	Quill- and beadwork, wampum belts

Iroquois religion

Spiritual life was an essential part of the Iroquois view of the world. A group of men and women priests, called the "Keepers of the Faith," organized ceremonies and rituals. In these rituals the shamans, or medicine men, would put on masks and dance, waving rattles and sprinkling tobacco. The shamans also performed secret ceremonies for curing illness. The Iroquois believed illness was caused by evil spirits and that the spirits of human beings were linked to forces of nature. They also believed that each person could fight evil spirits by using his or her own spiritual power, or orenda. Even though each person's orenda was small, it added to the total good spirit of the family group.

The Iroquois valued bravery very highly and believed that when warriors were killed, their deaths should be avenged by their clans or family groups, who were named after animals such as the wolf, the deer, and the turtle. The clan members would take an enemy prisoner and test his bravery and orenda (spiritual power) by submitting him to painful physical ordeals. These customs gave rise to a cycle of violent disputes between tribes that threatened to destroy the unity of the Iroquois League.

Curriculum Context

The naming of clans after animals is an example of how Native American attitudes toward nature are reflected in their traditions and practices.

The Great Law of Peace
Eventually an elder from the Huron tribe called Deganawida intervened in the conflict, preaching a message of peace. He was helped by an Onondaga shaman called Hiawatha.

Together, Deganawida and Hiawatha developed a set of laws by which the tribes could live together in peace and unity. Through their teaching they even succeeded in converting the warlike Onondaga priest Thadodaho, who was depicted in Iroquois legends as a monstrous figure with snakes for hair, hands like turtle claws, and the feet of a bear.

The Great Law of Peace, as the teaching came to be called, was recorded in pictures and symbols on

Great Law of Peace

A set of laws recorded on a series of wampum belts, laying down the founding constitution of the Iroquois League.

beaded belts called wampum belts. Such belts were also later used to record treaties and in money dealings with white settlers.

Under the Great Law the tribes stopped fighting and viewed their territory as a giant longhouse, with the eastern door guarded by the Mohawk and the western door by the Seneca. In the middle were the Onondaga, the keepers of the fire. A system was developed in which the women of the clans selected clan mothers,

This engraving, from a painting by R.W. Weir, shows the Seneca war chief Sa-go-ye-wat-ha, also known as Red Jacket. During the American Revolution Red Jacket was a messenger for British officers and is said to have received a red jacket as a reward.

who in turn appointed male chiefs for each of the tribes. All the different chiefs then met together in a Grand Council.

Political structure

The founders of the United States based many of their ideas about democracy on the political structure of the Iroquois League. For example, in 1754 Benjamin Franklin's Albany Plan of Union for the British colonies took ideas from the Iroquois system of government. When the U.S. Constitution was drawn up in 1787, it also incorporated many of the political structures of the Iroquois League. Today the Iroquois League is recognized as one of the world's oldest democracies.

Trade with European allies

The Iroquois League's era of power lasted from the beginning of the 17th century to the end of the 18th century. During that time they traded fur pelts, especially beaver, first with the Dutch and then with the British. They obtained guns from their European allies and were able to attack and destroy the Huron and the Erie, who were rival groups. They became allies of the English, fighting against the French in a number of different wars between 1689 and 1763.

They kept a strong alliance with the British, mainly because of their close relationship with William Johnson, a trader who married an Iroquois woman. In the American Revolution, they fought on the British side.

Resettlement

The Iroquois League was finally defeated by the Americans in 1779, and its tribes were later settled in New York State, losing a huge part of their homelands in the process.

Curriculum Context

Students might choose to focus on the Iroquois system of government in order to understand its influence on the development of the U.S. Constitution.

Curriculum Context

The curriculum may ask students to describe ways in which Native Americans cooperated with the settlers, for example in the fur trade and in military alliances.

Micmac

The Micmac lived in eastern Canada. They probably migrated from the Great Lakes region to what are now the Canadian maritime provinces long before Europeans arrived on the continent. Living on or near the coast, the Micmac developed their own unique culture from the traditional hunter–gatherer way of life characteristic of eastern Woodland peoples.

Land and sea

Traditional Micmac life followed a pattern dictated by the seasonal availability of food. For much of the year—from spring until fall—the Micmac lived on the coast in villages lying between the sea and a river or stream. These sites provided them with the mainstay of their diet: fish, shellfish, and game animals, as well as the occasional seal and whale. In late summer the women gathered berries and dug up ground nuts. Some foods were dried for winter use.

As winter approached, the Micmac moved inland, once again establishing a campsite near a river or stream that provided an abundance of food, particularly fall runs of eels and migrating ducks and geese. In winter, the Micmac trapped moose, deer, beaver, bear, and caribou, or hunted them with bows and arrows.

Throughout the year nuclear families (small families made up of a husband and wife and their children) lived in birchbark wigwams, while extended families (larger families made up of several generations of relatives) sheltered in larger, rectangular birchbark structures. In winter additional protection from the cold was provided by placing mats and animal skins over the birchbark.

Sometimes a Micmac village was surrounded by a palisade—a fence of wooden stakes—to fortify it against enemy raids.

Political and social life

The Micmac nation was divided into seven districts. Each district had a chief, under whom local chiefs were in charge of specific territories. At the head of all these chiefs was the Grand Chief, or *sagamore*. The Micmac tribes came together to decide policies affecting the whole nation. These meetings were attended by local and district chiefs and by other men who were particularly respected in the community.

The Micmac were a warlike people whose enemies included the Mohawk and the Algonquian tribes of New England. They sometimes fought the Subarctic Inuit and Malecite too. Although they were aggressive, the Micmac adopted captured women and children into their own community.

Curriculum Context

Students learning about the practice of government in different societies might compare the Micmac system with the political institutions that emerged in the colonies.

This photograph shows the frame of a wigwam of the type built by Woodland peoples such as the Micmac. The frames were made from poles that were put into the ground, forming a circle. The poles were then bent into an arch and tied together at the top.

Feasts and family life

Feasts were an important part of Micmac life and were held for a variety of major and lesser events, such as the marriage of a daughter, a funeral, or a child's first tooth.

Micmac men often took more than one wife. The women prepared and gathered food, and made clothing and household objects such as reed baskets and woven mats. The men hunted and fished.

Decline in population

The Micmac suffered greatly from the arrival of the Europeans. Disease, alcohol, genocide (murder of a race), and loss of traditional lands all resulted in a staggering decline in the Micmac population.

The total number of Micmac people before the arrival of the Europeans is not known, but reports from early settlers, missionaries, and traders suggest they were a powerful and important tribe in the area. By 1850 the total Micmac population was a mere 3,000.

Political unions

In 1867 the federal government of Canada took over responsibility for the Micmac. But it was not until more than 100 years later that the Micmac and other peoples came together to establish effective political unions, such as the Union of Nova Scotia Indians and the Union of New Brunswick Indians, both formed in 1969.

The Micmac today

Today the Micmac are pursuing land claims and damages from the federal government and have had some success in reclaiming hunting and fishing rights.

The Micmac are becoming increasingly aware and proud of traditional practices such as powwows, or meetings, yet their lifestyle is a mix of the traditional and the modern.

Powwow

A gathering of Native Americans, often involving feasting and dancing. The word comes from the Narragansett word *powwaw*, meaning "shaman" or "magician."

Mississippians

The Mississippians, or Temple Mound Builders, lived on the rich floodplains of rivers in the Southeast. They were expert farmers who began to establish sizable ceremonial and trade centers with large populations. The largest of these, Cahokia, across the Mississippi River from present-day St. Louis, may have had a population as large as 30,000.

The most notable features of Mississippian sites are flat-topped earth mounds or pyramids. On top of these mounds stood temples built of mud and thatch, which were looked after by a special caste of priests. The mounds, together with smaller mounds that supported housing for the nobles, usually formed an inner sanctum, or sacred place, which was protected by palisades (fences built of stakes).

The Mississippians imported improved varieties of corn from Mexico about 700 CE. Outside their town centers there were cultivated fields and a number of small communities that depended on the larger ones for resources.

Two divisions

Mississippian culture had two main divisions: one was associated with the Siouan-speaking people of the eastern Woodland, and the other was a western tradition associated with the Southern Cult. The Southern Cult was strongest in the Caddoan-speaking areas of modern-day Texas, but it also spread across the South to Georgia and had some influence throughout the Mississippian area.

An ordered society

Mississippian culture was organized as a system of ranked hereditary positions with a male leader or chief, who also acted as the high priest. It was believed that

> **Curriculum Context**
>
> The earth mounds or pyramids built by the Mississippians are good examples of structures that reflect the group's social organization as well as its religious beliefs and practices.

Curriculum Context

Students learning about the social organization of different groups might wish to focus on the hierarchical structure of Mississippian society.

he obtained his position through divine sanction. However, he inherited his power from his mother's side, and it was essential that she was of noble birth. Below the chief or high priest was a class of aristocrats, and below them were various honored professionals. Most of the population were commoners—a kind of working class—and beneath them were slaves, who were often captives from enemy groups.

Southern Cult artifacts

Human sacrifice was a familiar theme in the arts of the Southern Cult, which performed ceremonies at major

A Mississippian mound at Etowah, Georgia. The mound is one of a group of large mounds built after about 950 CE and abandoned by about 1600. The mounds contained grave goods that suggested they were built by members of the Southern Cult.

sites and became fully developed after 1000 CE. Human sacrifice is depicted on sculpture, pottery, masks, copper sheets, and gorgets (throat armor) from Southern Cult sites. Pots often take the form of the severed heads of captives, with the eyes and lips sewn shut. Other images include hunchbacked female figures and pipes in the shape of animals and birds. Also depicted are stylized symbols—skulls, bones, elaborate crosses, and the form of a weeping eye—that seem to be specifically associated with the practices and beliefs of the Southern Cult.

Most of the major Mississippian sites were abandoned before the period of European contact. Many reasons have been suggested for the decline of the Mississippian culture, including overpopulation, crop failure, and political strife.

The last surviving remnant of Mississippian culture was still being practiced by the Natchez when they were encountered by Hernando de Soto, a Spanish conquistador, or conqueror, in 1542. It continued until the Natchez were defeated in the 1730s by French soldiers and Choctaw mercenaries. The remaining Natchez fled as refugees to live among their former enemies, the Chickasaw, Creek, and Cherokee peoples.

Mohawk

The Mohawk played an important role in the Iroquois League of Nations. As the most eastern of the groups of the league they were known as the Guardians of the Eastern Door. They were responsible for preventing enemy attacks undermining the league's hold over the Mohawk Valley in New York. They were also known as the Receivers of Tribute.

The Mohawk were feared by most other native peoples and derive their name from the Algonquian word *Mohowauuck*, which means "they eat live things" or "man-eaters." They earned this reputation because although the Mohawk were the smallest tribe in the league, they were also the most aggressive.

This was evident in 1648 when the Mohawk, with Seneca allies, broke a truce with another powerful Iroquois tribe, the Huron. Inside a year the greatly outnumbered Mohawk and Seneca warriors defeated the Huron and forced them to seek protection as refugees among other tribes. But the Mohawk could also be generous and forgiving, and they invited many of the refugees to found their own villages in Mohawk territory under Mohawk protection.

Allies of the British

During the French and Indian War, as well as in the American Revolution, European nations and colonials vied with each other for Mohawk support. Most Mohawk were consistently friendly to the British and hostile to the French and Americans. Their famous leader, Thayendaneken, or Joseph Brant, was even made a commissioned officer in the British army during the late 18th century.

With British support the Mohawk established communities in Ontario, free of American influence.

Curriculum Context

Students learning about the alliances formed between Native American groups and the British could study the role of Joseph Brant in the American Revolution.

From an Original Drawing in the Possession of James Boswell Esq.

JOSEPH THAYENDANEKEN

The Mohawk Chief

Joseph Brant, for example, built a house at British expense, founding the town of Brantford. By being friendly with neighboring communities and adopting refugees from other groups, the Mohawk thrived in Ontario. Their present population there of about 10,000 is perhaps twice the size of the original tribe.

The Mohawk also continue to enjoy their reputation for fearlessness. Today a high proportion of the iron- and construction workers on the skyscrapers of New York City are Mohawk.

Joseph Thayendaneken, or Joseph Brant, the Mohawk chief, portrayed in 1776 by George Romney. Brant commanded the Iroquois forces for the British during the American Revolution and became a colonel in the British Army.

Mohegan

The Mohegan are sometimes confused with another native people called the Mahican. The confusion arose following the publication in 1826 of a popular novel, *The Last of the Mohicans*, written by James Fenimore Cooper. It is not clear which of the two groups, the Mahican or the Mohegan, the author actually meant by "Mohican," but in any case his book is a work of fiction.

Historical records show that the Mohegan and the Mahican were two related groups of Algonquian people. The original homelands of the Mohegan were around Connecticut. The Mahican lived along the northern end of the Hudson Valley—mainly in the present-day state of New York but also in Massachusetts and Vermont. Many Algonquian bands and villages near the Hudson River were united in a political grouping called the Mahican Confederacy.

Breakaway group

The Mohegan were an offshoot of the Pequot, a powerful, warlike tribe whose name is Algonquian for "destroyers." During the 17th century, the Pequot competed with other Algonquian peoples for control of southern New England, where lush forests and quiet bays made hunting and fishing easy.

The Last of the Mohicans

The Last of the Mohicans is set in 1757, during the French and Indian War. It tells the story of Natty Bumppo, a frontiersman, whose best friend is Chingachgook, a Native American brave. Chingachgook is the last surviving member of his tribe, the "Mohican." James Fenimore Cooper's adventure story—which has twice been made into a movie—captures the spirit of the Native American Northeast but is not historically accurate.

By 1620, when the Pilgrims landed at Plymouth Rock, the Pequot had gained control of the area under their chief, Sassacus. Sassacus lived in a village on the Thames River, and under him were 26 lower chiefs, each with his own village. One of these lower chiefs, Uncas, broke away from the Pequot and formed his own group of supporters. This group became known as the Mohegan.

Traditional way of life

At the beginning of the 17th century the Mohegan had a way of life that was similar to most of the other Algonquian peoples in the Northeast at that time. Their staple diet was fish, and they traveled by birchbark canoes.

However, the Mohegan way of life soon changed as white settlers began to move into the area. The immigrants fought against the Native Americans in the Northeast in the Pequot War of 1636, defeating Sassacus. Uncas made alliances with the Europeans, but finally they turned against him and his people too. The victorious immigrants took away the Mohegan's land and sold many of the Mohegan into slavery. Other Mohegan died from European diseases, such as smallpox.

Today the Mohegan, together with the Pequot, live on two small reservations in Connecticut and New York. To try to regain their homelands, the Mohegan filed a land claim and lawsuit against the state of Connecticut in the early 1980s. However, it was vetoed by President Ronald Reagan. Today the Mohegan are seeking funds to help improve their poor standard of living and maintain their culture.

Curriculum Context

The curriculum may ask students to describe how European contact affected native societies. Sassacus and Uncas had different ideas about how to deal with European settlers. The dispute led to Uncas forming a separate group.

Pequot War

A conflict in 1636–1637 between an alliance of English colonists and the Mohegan and Narragansett against the Pequot under their chief, Sassacus. The conflict resulted in the defeat of the Pequot.

Natchez

The Natchez of the Lower Mississippi Valley were members of the Temple Mound cultures of the Southeast. When Hernando de Soto's Spanish expedition came across them in 1542, the Natchez occupied nine villages and exerted wide influence and cultural leadership over neighboring groups.

Curriculum Context

Students learning about the religious beliefs and traditions of Pre-Contact groups might focus on the burial practices of the Natchez.

Hernando de Soto noted that the Natchez chief, or Great Sun, lived in a large cabin built on top of a long mound in their principal village. Close by was a second mound topped by a "sun temple" in which the bones of previous Great Suns were laid to rest. In this temple priests tended a fire that was permanently kept alight.

The Natchez were farmers, with fields of corn, millet, melons, pumpkins, sunflowers, and tobacco. However,

This illustration shows Hernando de Soto, leader of a Spanish expedition to the Southeast. This was the first European expedition to reach the Mississippi and make contact with the Natchez.

they were also warlike and had societies of warriors who wore distinctive tattooed markings and hairstyles that symbolized the various brotherhoods to which they belonged.

European deceit

The Natchez chief Quigualtam, who was Great Sun at the time of de Soto's visit, claimed direct descent from the sun. Having heard rumors of Quigualtam's supposed ancestry, de Soto declared himself to be the sun's younger brother. De Soto's deceit was discovered when Quigualtam demanded proof by asking him to dry up the Mississippi River. When de Soto failed to do this, the Natchez drove the Spanish from their lands.

As the Great Sun, Quigualtam enjoyed absolute authority by divine sanction (the will of the gods).

Curriculum Context

The distinctive tattoos and hairstyles of the Natchez are good examples of ways in which native groups reflected their tribal identities through different forms of body adornment.

Natchez

Language:	Natchez (Muskogean or possibly Algonquian)
Area:	Lower Mississippi Valley
Reservation:	None
Population:	Nearly 4,000 in 1700; none by 1800
Housing:	Large villages with temple mounds
European contact:	Spanish forces in 1542 and French at the end of the 17th century
Neighbors:	Choctaw, Chickasaw
Lifestyle:	Farmers, but warlike, with rigid class system
Food:	Mainly corn, fruit, and vegetables, plus some fish and game
Crafts:	Pottery, basketry, weaving, and matting

He was believed to have inherited this from his mother, since in the Natchez descent system power passed from the females of the Sun class. Beneath the Suns was a class of nobles and below them were "honored people" who could achieve rank through bravery in war or other exemplary acts.

Death rituals

Male captives were usually tortured to death. During the torture they were expected to sing death songs in defiance of their captors as a show of their bravery. However, a young woman who had lost her husband in war could ask for a prisoner to be pardoned so he could take the place of the dead man.

Curriculum Context

A comparative study of death rituals and beliefs about the afterlife will help students understand the similarities and differences between Native American cultures.

Natchez society was dominated by death rituals. At the burial of a Great Sun his wives and other close relatives offered to be strangled so that they could accompany him in the afterlife. Commoners might kill their babies and young children as sacrifices, throwing the bodies beneath the feet of the priests and litter-bearers who carried the Great Sun's body to its final resting place in the temple. Natchez society recognized the extremity of this act by elevating to the status of noble any commoner who sacrificed a child.

Relations with the French

By the end of the 17th century the Natchez had established friendly relations with the French, whose traders and missionaries were active in the region.

Curriculum Context

The curriculum may ask students to evaluate the reasons for the changing relationships between Native Americans and European settlers.

These relations soured early in 1716. That year the French established Fort Rosalie near the main Natchez village, and the commandant, Chépart, demanded the site of the village for his own plantation.

Natchez warriors surrounded Chépart in his cabin, but the Frenchman pleaded so pitifully for his life that the disgusted warriors refused to dirty their weapons with the blood of a coward. Instead, they appointed a commoner to beat him to death with a stick.

French retaliation was swift. They secured the assistance of Choctaw and Tunica allies and marched on the Natchez villages. However, the Natchez were warned, and the French found the villages abandoned.

Conflict and defeat

By 1729, after years of French intimidation, the Natchez led a general uprising. Two hundred Frenchmen were killed, their wives and children captured, and Fort Rosalie burned to the ground. With Choctaw support the Natchez attacked New Orleans, but at the last moment the Choctaw defected and joined the French again who, with other Native American allies, scattered the Natchez. Four hundred captured men, women, and children were sold by the French into slavery in the West Indies. By the end of the fighting in 1732 the Natchez had been reduced to only 100 warriors. Fifty years earlier they could easily have fielded 1,500.

French revenge was so complete that the Natchez no longer exist as a people. Scattered bands sought refuge among the Chickasaw, Creek, and Cherokee and became members of these tribes. One small group did maintain an independent existence for a time, at Four Hole Swamp in South Carolina. However, the site was abandoned in 1744 after Natchez warriors killed seven Catawba Native Americans and then fled in fear of Catawba revenge.

Curriculum Context

In a study of the survival strategies of Native American societies, students might concentrate on the resistance of the Natchez and the reasons for their defeat.

Ojibway

The Ojibway, known also as the Ojibwa, Chippewa, or Chippeway, live in the Great Lakes region. Their hunting grounds once stretched all the way from Montana and Saskatchewan in the west as far east as southern Ontario. Originally they lived in the St. Lawrence region of eastern Canada before migrating southwest in prehistoric times. Records of these early journeys are preserved on sacred birchbark scrolls.

Around the time of their first contact with Europeans, in the late 16th century, the Ojibway population stood at 35,000 and formed the largest Native American group north of Mexico. Today they are still the largest alliance of tribes in North America. The people speak various dialects of the Algonquian language. Many Ojibway refer to themselves as *Anishinaabe*, which means "the first people."

Curriculum Context

The forms of transportation used by the Ojibway are a good example of how native groups adjusted to their environment. Their canoes were ideal for travel and fishing in the lakes, streams, and rivers of the Great Lakes region.

Great Lakes lifestyle

The Great Lakes region is dotted with lakes and crisscrossed by numerous streams and rivers. The Ojibway traditionally used canoes to travel their territory and were expert canoe-builders, stitching sheets of birchbark over wooden frames and sealing the edges with spruce gum.

The artist and explorer George Catlin, who visited the region in the first half of the 19th century, wrote: "The bark canoe of the Chippeways is, perhaps, the most beautiful and light model of all the water crafts that ever were invented. They are so ingeniously shaped and sewed together… that they ride upon the water, as light as a cork." In the snowy north the Ojibway used toboggans pulled by dogs to haul their supplies.

The Ojibway were mainly forest dwellers who moved between summer and winter camps, living in domed shelters covered with bark, thatch, or hides. They speared fish, hunted game, and picked berries and other wild plants. The Ojibway who lived in the south also raised crops and lived a more settled life.

Ojibway food

Wild rice was a staple part of the Ojibway diet. The rice grew in wetlands on the margins of lakes. The Ojibway harvested the rice early in the fall by canoe, then threshed it with sticks to separate the kernels from the husks. In spring the Ojibway tapped maple trees, boiled and strained the sweet sap, then stirred it as it crystallized into maple sugar. They ate the sugar, along with fruit, vegetables, cereals, and even fish, throughout the year.

The harvesting and preparation of wild rice and maple sugar were social gatherings at which people told

Ojibway

Language:	Ojibway, an Algonquian language
Area:	Great Lakes region: Quebec, Ontario, Minnesota, and Michigan
Reservation:	Great Lakes region
Population:	35,000 in 1600; over 100,000 today
Housing:	Domed shelters covered with bark, thatch, or hides
European contact:	French explorers in the late 16th century
Neighbors:	Iroquois, Cree, Menominee, Huron, Ottawa, and Sioux
Lifestyle:	Forest dwellers who traveled the rivers in birchbark canoes
Food:	Wild rice, berries, and other wild plants; fish and game
Crafts:	Birchbark pictures, bark containers, quillwork, and beadwork

The Ojibway are the largest original Native American nation in the Great Lakes region.

stories and swapped gossip. On winter evenings, people also grouped around the fire to tell stories as they made pictures on thin birchbark or made bark containers and decorated them with beads or feathers.

Midewiwin

A medicine society important among the Ojibway. Its members perform curing rituals, using healing herbs and mysticism to promote physical and spiritual well-being.

The Midewiwin is a medicine society that was important among the Ojibway and was adopted by other local peoples. It stresses harmony with nature and the use of healing herbs. It takes many years for trainees to learn the healing properties of herbs and understand the society's ideas. The society still has many members.

Allies and enemies

From prehistoric times the Ojibway competed with other tribes for hunting grounds. Traditional enemies included the Fox, Sioux, and Iroquois, and clashes with these groups continued into historic times. In the 1600s the Ojibway fought the Iroquois and drove them from their lands in southeast Ontario and Michigan. In the 1600s and 1700s they fought the Fox and drove the Sioux from Minnesota.

Curriculum Context

Curricula often ask students to examine the reasons why Native American groups formed alliances with European settlers in the 1600s and 1700s.

The first contact the Ojibway had with Europeans was through French fur traders, who entered the Great Lakes region in the 1550s. Lone French explorers called *voyageurs* used canoes to reach remote areas and trade with the Ojibway and other Native Americans, exchanging guns, knives, tools, and liquor for fur. In the 1600s the British arrived in search of land to settle, and in the 1700s they clashed with French forces. The Ojibway and other Native Americans sometimes sided with the colonial powers when it served their interests.

However, the Ojibway mainly fought against the Europeans in the 1700s in order to defend their lands. In 1755 they allied with other tribes to defeat the British, under General Braddock, near Pittsburgh. In 1763 they joined the Ottawa, led by Chief Pontiac, against British forces at the Siege of Detroit. When the United States gained possession of the Great Lakes region in 1803, through the Louisiana Purchase, the Ojibway allied with the Shawnee, under Tecumseh, to fight the U.S. Army.

Throughout most of the 19th century the Ojibway continued to resist settlement of their lands and attempts by the United States to force them onto reservations. Their last battle with the U.S. Army was at Leach Lake in Minnesota in 1898.

Ojibway today

Today some 100,000 Ojibway live in bands or on reservations scattered over the Great Lakes region. Two-thirds of them live in Canada, and about 10 percent speak a dialect of Ojibway. Their communities include many who are not Native Americans but people of mixed heritage.

Ojibway councils support economic growth and defend their historic traditions, such as fishing rights. Recently some Ojibway have been acclaimed as writers, including the poet Gerald Vizenor and the prize-winning novelist Louise Erdrich.

Curriculum Context

Students learning about the effects of the policy of removal may be asked to examine the survival strategies of different Native American groups. The Ojibway adopted a policy of resistance.

Osage

Long before Europeans first began to explore inland America, the Osage were living in villages along the Missouri River. They irrigated the valleys to grow corn, gathered fruit, and hunted game in the forests. Twice every year the Osage journeyed to the northern Plains to hunt buffalo. In the valleys the people lived in large earth lodges by streams and rivers. On buffalo hunts the Osage sheltered in tepees like the Plains peoples.

Roach

A hairstyle in which the head is shaved except for a strip from front to back across the top of the head.

Osage clothing

The Osage dressed in clothes made from deerskin and other hides. The men wore loincloths, leggings, and moccasins, and buffalo hide or bearskin robes in cold weather. The women wore leggings and dresses belted with bands of woven buffalo hair. Both men and women decorated their bodies with tattoos and donned earrings and bracelets. The men wore their hair in a roach. The women wore their hair loose.

Contact with Europeans

In the 1670s French explorers navigating downriver from their lands in New France made first contact with the Osage, near the Osage River in modern-day Missouri. The Osage began trading with the French, exchanging furs for horses and guns. With these new possessions the Osage dominated the other native peoples of the territory for 100 years.

Curriculum Context

Many curricula ask students to examine the alliances that Native Americans made with colonists from different nations and the effects of these alliances on their societies.

When the French influence in the region waned, the Osage allied with the Spanish. In the late 18th century the fur trade caused a division within the Osage, and half the people left to settle in what is now Arkansas.

Land sales and reservations

In 1804 the Lewis and Clark expedition encountered the Osage while mapping the unknown lands of the

West for the U.S. government. The explorers estimated the Osage population at 6,500. When white settlers reached the Missouri and Arkansas territories, the Osage negotiated with the newcomers.

Between 1808 and 1825 the Osage sold most of their lands to the whites and were moved onto a reservation farther west, in what is now Kansas. There they fought on the side of the Union in the Civil War (1861–1865), and many Osage married white settlers.

In 1871 the U.S. government made the Osage sell their Kansas lands for $8 million. The Osage were moved again, this time to a larger reserve in the Indian Territory. There they leased their pasture lands to Texas ranchers who needed to graze their cattle as they drove them north to the railroads of Kansas. With this income and the interest from the sale of the Kansas lands, the Osage prospered.

Curriculum Context

Students might be asked to explore the role of the U.S. government's federal Indian policy in the transformation of agriculture and ranching in the 19th century.

Osage

Language:	Siouan–Dhegiha
Area:	Missouri and Arkansas
Reservation:	None
Population:	2,200 in 1906, approximately 10,000 today
Housing:	Earth lodges and tepees
European contact:	French explorers in the 1670s, Spanish colonists in the 1700s
Neighbors:	Kiowa, Wichita, Kansa, Missouri, Quapaw, and Caddo
Lifestyle:	Farmers and buffalo-hunters of the Plains
Food:	Game, corn, and fruit
Crafts:	Weaving and skin tanning

The discovery of oil and gas on their lands in the 1900s made many of the Osage wealthy.

Children of the middle waters

The Osage called themselves the "children of the middle waters." They believed their world was formed when the Creator changed the middle waters into air, earth, and water. This same world view was echoed in Osage society, which was divided into two groups. Some were said to descend from Earth People, others from Sky People. The Sky Chief led the Osage in times of peace, and the Earth Chief in times of war.

In the late 1880s Congress abolished the Indian Territory and created a new state, Oklahoma. Reservation lands held communally by Native American groups were to be divided up and allotted to individuals. Native Americans would receive 160 acres (65 ha) each—the rest of the land went to white settlers and developers. The Osage resisted this new policy and in 1906 they were given over 500 acres (200 ha) each and allowed to hold communal mineral rights to their lands.

Curriculum Context

In 1887 the Dawes General Allotment Act distributed reservation land to individual Native American households. The curriculum may ask students to compare the effects of this policy on different groups.

Wealth and prosperity

In the early 1900s it was discovered that the Osage lands were rich in oil and natural gas. Oil drilling began in 1904. By the 1920s revenues from oil and gas had made the Osage famous as "the richest group of people in the world." The new wealth helped the Osage retain their independence and identity as a people.

During the 20th century the fortunes of the Osage rose and fell with the price of oil on the world market. The Osage population, which fell to 1,500 in the 1880s, now stands at about 10,000 and continues to grow year by year.

Pawnee

Several hundred years before Europeans first visited inland America, the Pawnee moved to the Plains, probably from the Southwest. There they ranged over the lands between the Platte and Missouri rivers. In the 1500s the Pawnee were one of the first native groups to gain horses from European explorers. The group quickly became fine horse riders and breeders.

The Pawnee speak several dialects of the Caddoan language, which may have been related in ancient times to that of the Iroquois. Today very few people speak the Pawnee language.

Lifestyle of the Pawnee

In winter, the Pawnee lived in circular earth lodges with timber walls and domed roofs. In summer, they followed the buffalo and lived in tepees. The Pawnee grew corn, squash, pumpkins, and other crops. They gathered wild plants and berries in the hills and valleys.

Pawnee men wore their hair in a roach. Both men and women pierced their ears and wore earrings, necklaces, and other ornaments.

Tribal organization

Pawnee society was made up of groups called bands. Each band was led by a council of local chiefs, religious leaders, and experienced warriors. The council made decisions about hunts, ceremonies, and warfare.

The Louisiana Purchase

In 1803, through the Louisiana Purchase, the United States gained vast pieces of land in the Midwest, including much of the Plains. From this time the Pawnee began to make treaties with the United States. As early as 1806 two Pawnee delegates traveled to Washington to represent their people.

Curriculum Context

A comparative study of how different Native American groups obtained food will help students learn how climate and geography affected their lifestyles.

Louisiana Purchase

The purchase by the United States from France in 1803 of 828,000 square miles (2,144,000 sq km) of land, comprising the western part of the Mississippi valley, including the modern-day states of Louisiana, Missouri, Arkansas, Iowa, Nebraska, North Dakota, South Dakota, and Oklahoma. The purchase doubled the size of the United States.

By the mid-1800s the Pawnee had given up most of their lands and were moved onto a reservation in Nebraska. In 1875 they were moved again, this time to the Indian Territory, the area west of the Mississippi where the government settled many Native American peoples. On these reservations the culture of the Pawnee weakened, and their traditions began to die away.

Disenfranchisement

In the early 1800s the Pawnee population was estimated at 12,000. However, during the 19th century the population fell rapidly because of diseases such as cholera and smallpox, poor living conditions, and raids by the Sioux and other warring groups.

The white settlers' greed for land caused the Pawnee further suffering. In 1887 a new law called the Dawes

Dawes General Allotment Act

A U.S. law passed in 1887 to divide up reservation lands and provide individual Native American households with an allotment of land to farm.

Pawnee

Language:	Hokan-Caddoan
Area:	Great Plains: Kansas and Nebraska
Reservation:	Indian Territory but abolished in the 1880s
Population:	12,000 in the early 1800s; approximately 2,500 today
Housing:	Earth lodges and tepees
European contact:	Francisco de Coronado in 1541
Neighbors:	Sioux, Arapaho, Kiowa-Apache, Wichita, Omaha, and Kansa
Lifestyle:	Farmers and buffalo-hunters
Food:	Corn and other crops, wild plants, and buffalo meat
Crafts:	Basketry, tanning, and quillwork

The Pawnee have roamed the Great Plains since prehistoric times.

Ceremony and beliefs

The Pawnee had a well-developed religion that was distinct from that of other local peoples. The main element of many ceremonies was the Sacred Bundles. These holy objects helped the people have good relations with the Sacred Beings in the heavens and with the plants and animals of the Earth. Many Pawnee rituals continued into the 20th century, but now only the Young Dog Dance and the Kitkehahki War Dance are still performed.

General Allotment Act set out to divide up the lands given to tribal peoples. Native Americans were each to receive an allotment of 160 acres (65 ha). The rest of the land was given to white settlers. The Pawnee resisted the policy, but in vain.

By 1892 the lands that had been reserved for the Pawnee by the U.S. government only 15 years before, and which were intended to remain theirs forever, were divided. The Indian Territory was broken up, and the state of Oklahoma was created.

By 1900 there were only about 600 Pawnee left. Today the Pawnee number about 2,500. About 400 live in Pawnee, Oklahoma, and every July the town hosts the Pawnee Homecoming.

Curriculum Context

The curriculum may ask students to understand the provisions of the Dawes General Allotment Act and evaluate its effects on tribal identity and land ownership.

Sauk and Fox

The Sauk and Fox joined together in the 18th century after most of the Fox were killed in battles with the French. Both peoples came from the Midwest—the Sauk from the Wisconsin River area, and the Fox from Illinois. Both spoke Algonquian and had a similar way of life. They lived in permanent villages, in lodges covered with elm bark. In summer they tended crops, while in winter they hunted game.

The Fox were one of the few Algonquian-speaking groups who were hostile toward the French. This was partly because the French were allies of the Ojibway (Chippewa), who were longtime enemies of the Fox. Together, the French and the Ojibway attacked the Fox, driving them out of their homelands. By 1734 there were so few Fox left that they joined with the neighboring Sauk.

Losing homelands

At the beginning of the 19th century some Sauk and Fox members signed away their tribal lands in Illinois in an agreement with the U.S. government. Under Chief Keokuk they agreed to move to lands in Iowa. Other Sauk and Fox claimed that this agreement was made without their knowledge.

Led by Chief Black Hawk, these other Sauk and Fox refused to leave their homelands. Black Hawk was helped by a shaman from the Winnebego named White Cloud, who gained support from other groups such as the Winnebego, Kickapoo, and Potawatomi.

When Black Hawk and his followers left their village to go hunting in the winter, white settlers moved in. From then on there was conflict between the rebel Sauk and Fox and the U.S. Army. Black Hawk's group was finally defeated on August 3, 1832. Black Hawk

This 1838 lithograph shows the Sauk and Fox chief Keokuk, with a child seated at his feet. Keokuk's agreement with the government to move the tribes from Illinois led Black Hawk to rebel and fight.

surrendered and was put in prison. He was later released but died in 1838, having failed to protect his people's homelands. After his death, grave robbers removed his body from his tomb and displayed his head in a traveling show.

Under Keokuk the remaining Sauk and Fox people were forced to move, first to Kansas and then to the Indian Territory, in what is now Oklahoma. Although today the two groups are often referred to together they officially divided in 1854.

Tribal names

The Native American name for the Fox is *Mesquaki* or *Muskwaki*. The name means "red earth people" and refers to the color of the ground in their homelands. When the Mesquaki came into contact with the French in the 17th century, the French mistakenly called the whole group by one of their clan names, *Wagosh*, meaning "fox." The Sauk, who are also known as the Sac, got their name from the Algonquian word meaning "yellow earth people."

Seminole

The Seminole migrated during the early 1700s from Georgia to Florida, which at the time was controlled by the Spanish. Many of these people were escaping slavery in the British-controlled northern colonies. They settled in the Everglades area, bravely defending their way of life and their independence over a period of almost 200 years.

The Seminole were mostly from the Creek group, but they were also joined by other native peoples, such as the Yuchi, Uamasee, and Choctaw.

The name Seminole comes from the Creek word *Simanóle*, meaning "separatist" or "runaway," and describes a people who made their home in the swamps. They were joined by many Native American war refugees and runaway African slaves. The Seminole hid the slaves and welcomed them into their families. Over the years these Africans married into the group and became known as "Black Seminole."

Seminole lifestyle

The Seminole were fishers and hunters. They also gathered fruit, nuts, and berries. Once settled, they became farmers, growing corn, sugarcane, guava, and bananas. They also raised cattle and horses.

Chickee

A Seminole house built on stilts, with a log frame, open sides, and a thatched roof over a raised wooden platform. *Chickee* is the Seminole word for house.

The Seminole lived in houses called *chickees*, which were ideally suited to the warm, wet conditions of the Florida swamps. These houses were high enough out of the water to stay dry and they had open sides to let in cool air.

For transport the Seminole made dugout canoes with a platform at the back. A person could stand on this platform and push the boat with a long pole that reached to the bottom of the swamp.

War with the United States

In 1812 the Seminole learned that some slaveowners from Georgia were planning to raid their settlements. To preempt this raid, they attacked the Georgians on their own plantations. The U.S. government then sent troops into Florida, led by General Andrew Jackson, who became known to Native Americans as "sharp knife." General Jackson's troops looted and burned native villages. In 1816 forces under General Edmund Gaines attacked a settlement of Black Seminole and killed most of the inhabitants, taking the survivors back as slaves. The following year the First Seminole War (1817–1818) began when Jackson again crossed the border and destroyed more Seminole villages.

The United States bought Florida from the Spanish in 1819. Settlers soon began to move into the area and

Seminole canoes on the Miami River in 1904. The Seminole made canoes from hollowed-out cypress logs.

to drive out the Native Americans. On May 28, 1830, the Indian Removal Act was passed, forcing many native groups onto reservations in the Indian Territory (present-day Oklahoma).

The first groups to be moved to the Indian Territory were the so-called Five Civilized Tribes: the Seminole, Choctaw, Creek, Chickasaw, and Cherokee. They were called "civilized" because, like Europeans and Americans, they lived in villages and farmed.

Trail of Tears

The removal of the Five Tribes became known as the Trail of Tears. Thousands of Native Americans were forced by troops to move to the land reserved for them in the Indian Territory. But the Seminole fiercely resisted being forced off their lands, and this resistance led to the Second Seminole War (1835–1842).

Curriculum Context

In a study of the impact of the Indian Removal Act, students might choose to focus on the consequences of the Trail of Tears and the Seminole policy of resistance.

Seminole

Language:	Muskogean
Area:	Florida
Reservation:	Southern Florida and Oklahoma
Population:	100,000 Pre-Contact; approximately 13,800 today
Housing:	Chickees, swamp pole-and-thatch houses
European contact:	Spanish conquistadors in 16th century; European settlers in 18th century
Neighbors:	Creek, Choctaw, and Chickasaw
Lifestyle:	Fishing, hunting, and gathering
Food:	Fish, shellfish, corn, wild fruit, and small game
Crafts:	Patchwork and appliqué clothing

The Seminole lived in the Everglades and maintained their independence for almost 200 years.

This lithograph drawn in 1838 shows Osceola, leader of the Seminole in the Second Seminole War. Osceola was not a hereditary chief but had risen to lead his people because of his brave stand against white settlers.

The Second Seminole War

The leader of the Seminole at this time was Chief Osceola. With a small band of warriors he defeated U.S. troops at Withlacoochee in Citrus County. The army then lured Osceola and his advisers to a peace meeting and captured them. Osceola died in prison, but two of his men, Wild Cat and John Horse, escaped. The army troops who pursued them were ambushed and defeated by Seminole. Further battles ensued, and the war dragged on until 1842, costing the U.S. government many lives and over 20 million dollars.

The Third Seminole War

In 1855 the Third Seminole War (1855–1858) broke out when Seminole chief Billy Bowlegs attacked the U.S.

military in Collier County. This time the war lasted for three years. At the end of this period most of the Seminole had been forced onto the Indian Territory, and only a few remained in the Everglades. In the Indian Territory, the Seminole came into conflict with the Creek. There was not enough land or food for both groups, and resentments grew.

The situation was made worse in 1887 when the Dawes General Allotment Act was passed. The act declared that only individuals, not tribes, could own land and that settlers could buy any remaining land. These rules created conflict among the tribes, and much native land eventually ended up in the hands of settlers.

Indian Reorganization Act

Legislation passed June 18, 1934, also known as the Indian New Deal. It attempted to give new rights to Native Americans living on reservations, reversing the Dawes General Allotment Act and restoring self-government on a tribal basis.

In 1934 the Indian Reorganization Act was passed to try to improve life for Native Americans. Under the act, many tribes formed their own councils with their own constitutions and were given government aid for the provision of health care, education, and cultural projects.

In 1957 the Seminole Tribe of Florida was formally created. However, those Seminole who spoke the Mikosuki language split away from this group to form the Miccosukee Tribe of Florida. Today both groups have reservations in Florida and in Oklahoma.

Shawnee

The traditional homelands of the Shawnee are in the Southeast, around the Cumberland Basin of the Tennessee River and on the Savannah River in South Carolina. The group's name comes from the Algonquian word *Shawunogi*, meaning "Southerners." Like their close linguistic relatives, the Sauk, Fox, and Kickapoo, they were a nomadic people.

Sites of Shawnee villages have been found along rivers in Tennessee, Kentucky, Ohio, and Virginia. Perhaps no other tribe divided and moved so frequently.

Allies and enemies
Although they were only a small tribe, the Shawnee formed alliances with many other groups. At various times they were allies of the Miami, Delaware, Ottawa, and Potawatomi.

Between 1689 and 1763 the Shawnee were allies of the French in the long wars with the British. After the wars the British promised the Shawnee land, but the governor of Virginia, Lord Dunmore, refused to honor the promise. The Shawnee went to war with the Virginians, but were defeated in 1774.

War with the Americans
When the American Revolution began in 1775, the Shawnee supported the British. When the Americans won the war, the Shawnee again had to resist an influx of new settlers onto their lands. The Shawnee resisted these incursions but they were finally defeated at the Battle of Fallen Timbers in 1794.

A great leader
Tecumseh and Tenskwataw were two Shawnee brothers who shared a vision of a united Native American people. Tecumseh was probably the greatest

Curriculum Context

The curriculum may ask students to consider why some Native Americans remained loyal to the British in the American Revolution. The Shawnee believed the British would prevent further encroachments on their land by colonists.

War of 1812

A war (1812–1815) between the United States and Britain over trade restrictions introduced by Britain to impede U.S. trade with France. The war ended with the Treaty of Ghent and neither side was victorious.

native leader of his time and worked tirelessly to unite the tribes at a crucial point in their history. But the hopes of Tecumseh and his brother ended when U.S. troops destroyed the Shawnee settlement at Tippecanoe in 1811.

Tecumseh's anger against the Americans was so great that he fought for the British during the War of 1812. He became a brigadier-general but was killed on October 5, 1813, at the Battle of the Thames.

Worn down by constant resistance to Europeans and Americans, the Shawnee divided. Some fled to Texas and Kansas, while others joined the Creek confederacy. A few bands went to the Indian Territory (in present-day Oklahoma), but they settled in separate districts and lost any tribal group identity.

This 1833 lithograph depicts the death of Tecumseh at the Battle of the Thames in 1813.

Sioux

Until the 18th century, the Sioux lived in the Woodland region, surrounded by larger rival tribes. There were three main groups: the Santee (eastern), Yankton (central), and Teton (western). In the 18th century, conflict with the Ojibway (Chippewa) forced the Sioux, who together numbered around 25,000 at the time, to move to the buffalo ranges of the Great Plains.

The name Sioux derives from an Ojibway word for "enemy." The Santee, Yankton, and Teton Sioux referred to themselves respectively as Dakota, Nakota, and Lakota, or "allies." The Teton comprised seven subtribes: the Blackfoot, Brule, Oglala, Sans Arcs, Minniconjou, Two-Kettle, and Hunkpapa.

Life on the Plains

In the Woodland region the Sioux lived on deer, beans, and wild rice. On the Plains they lived a nomadic hunting lifestyle based on following the buffalo herds. The buffalo provided food, clothing, and shelter. They also traded, exchanging firearms and horses for tobacco and other goods from Great Lakes tribes.

The basic social and hunting unit of the Sioux was the band (an extended family group). Each band usually had more than one chief, respected men who offered advice but never gave orders. Decisions at a tribal level were made by a council of many chiefs.

Polygamy (having more than one wife) was common for men, but a warrior could marry only after he had proved himself in battle. Although they had no laws as such, the Sioux lived by a severe code of punishments. Adultery by women was punished by disfigurement. Men disobeying the hunting regulations had their tepees and property destroyed. Old people too weak to travel with the band were simply left to die.

Curriculum Context

Students asked to analyze the organization of Native American societies might wish to focus on the tribal organization and system of government of the Sioux.

Men in Plains tribes acquired status through acts of bravery in battle, and Sioux warriors were particularly renowned for their courage. They wore specially cut feathers in their hair to signify their deeds. The bravest deed was counting coup—touching an enemy with a special stick.

The Sioux and the Cree were the only Plains tribes to consider scalping as a first-class war honor. Bringing home a scalp not only demonstrated a warrior's success, it was also believed to "capture" the dead man's spirit. The spirit would then accompany the victor as a companion when he himself died and traveled to the afterworld.

Curriculum Context

The Sioux are a good example of a group that strongly resisted encroachments on their land by settlers.

Fighting for survival

Of all the Great Plains peoples the Sioux most fiercely resisted incursions by white Americans on their lands. In 1851 the U.S. government signed the first Treaty of

Sioux

In the 18th century the Sioux moved from the Woodland region to the Plains.

Language:	Siouan
Area:	Great Plains
Reservation:	North and South Dakota, Montana, and Nebraska
Population:	25,000 in 18th century; 40,000 today
Housing:	Tepees ("dwellings" in Siouan)
European contact:	French settlers in the 18th century
Neighbors:	Mandan, Crow, Cree, Cheyenne, Blackfoot, and Ojibway (Chippewa)
Lifestyle:	Nomadic buffalo hunters and warriors
Food:	Buffalo and other game animals
Crafts:	Bead embroidery, skinwork, and carving

Spiritual life of the Sioux

The Sioux believed in one all-powerful god, called Wakan Tanka, "the Great Spirit," who was present throughout the natural world. A Sioux man's most sacred possession was his tobacco pipe, without which no ceremony could take place. Tribally owned pipes, or calumets, were smoked before going into battle, when making peace with an enemy, to bring rain, and to ensure a successful buffalo hunt. Young Sioux men often went on Vision Quests to seek direction from the spirit of an animal. They went off alone into the wilderness and fasted (went without food or water). They then called on the spirit for guidance. They also painted likenesses of these spirits on their war shields to protect themselves in battle.

Fort Laramie with the Sioux and other tribes. This treaty assigned boundaries to each group. But the peace was not to last, and a pattern of raiding developed as white settlers cut across Sioux lands, killing buffalo on their way to Oregon and California.

Red Cloud's War and the Battle of Little Bighorn

Throughout the 1860s matters worsened as settlers tried to open the Bozeman Trail—a route to the gold fields in the Rockies—through the Sioux's favorite hunting grounds in the Bighorn Mountains. This was the trigger for Red Cloud's War (1865–1867). An Oglala Sioux chief, Red Cloud was the only Native American to lead a successful war against the U.S. Army. It ended with the second Fort Laramie Treaty of 1868, which guaranteed southern Dakota to the Sioux and the scrapping of the Bozeman Trail.

However, when gold was discovered in the Black Hills in the mid-1870s, thousands of miners ignored the treaty and swarmed onto the Sioux reservation with tacit army support. The conflict that followed ended with the Battle of Little Bighorn in 1876, where Sioux, Arapaho, and Cheyenne warriors, led by Sitting Bull and Crazy Horse, surrounded and killed Lieutenant Colonel George Custer and over 200 of his troops.

> **Curriculum Context**
>
> The curriculum may ask students to analyze the outcomes of the major treaties formed between the U.S. government and Native American groups.

This painting, created in about 1900 by the Sioux artist Amos Bad Heart Buffalo, shows Sioux warriors leading away captured horses after the defeat of Custer's troops at the Battle of Little Bighorn.

The spectacular victory was short-lived, and later that year the Sioux were forced to surrender and return to their reservations. Sitting Bull fled to Canada with several thousand followers but returned to the United States in 1881 and surrendered to the army.

Curriculum Context

The U.S. government's attitude toward the adoption of the Ghost Dance religion by the Sioux is important in understanding the factors that led to the massacre at Wounded Knee.

Ghost Dance religion and Wounded Knee
In 1890 a movement known as the Ghost Dance religion spread across the Plains, promising Native Americans the destruction of white Americans and the restocking of the Plains with buffalos. The movement took hold among the Sioux. The government feared it might provoke another uprising and came to arrest Sitting Bull, who was killed during a scuffle. Finally, the U.S. Army's massacre of about 250 Sioux men, women, and children at Wounded Knee that year marked the end of all Sioux resistance.

American Indian Movement (AIM)

A civil rights organization that seeks the restoration of original tribal lands and better treatment of Native Americans.

Battle for Sioux rights
Today there are more than 40,000 Sioux, most of whom live on reservations. In recent years many Sioux have been active in the American Indian Movement (AIM). In 1973 members of AIM occupied the town of Wounded Knee for 71 days and succeeded in provoking a U.S. Senate investigation into Native American living conditions.

Southeast/Florida Peoples

The Southeast forms a vast area that was home to dozens of tribes and powerful confederacies. The wet, humid, and densely wooded region is bordered by the Atlantic to the east, semitropical Florida and the Gulf of Mexico to the south and southwest, the Mississippi River to the west, and the Virginia–North Carolina coastal plain to the north.

This region was once home to North America's most advanced peoples, the Mound Builders, who were active west of the Appalachian Mountains between 1000 BCE and 1500 CE. They built thousands of mounds and earthworks during this period. There were two major cultures: Woodland to the north and Mississippian to the south.

Impressive settlements

Before the arrival of Europeans these peoples had a well-developed farming tradition. The ready availability of raw materials such as timber enabled them to build impressive towns and villages. Characteristically, these were palisaded, or fenced, and their centerpieces were flat-topped mounds for ceremonial temples.

The best-known Southeast tribes are the Five Civilized Tribes (the Cherokee, Choctaw, Chickasaw, Creek, and Seminole). These Southeast societies were hierarchical. Their elites of hereditary leaders wielded absolute power. They ruled tribute-levying chiefdoms until the Spanish conquistadors, or conquerors, Juan Ponce de León and Hernando de Soto arrived in the 16th century.

Everyday Southeast life

Homes varied, but many were conical and thatched with grass or bark. Others were cabins made of wood and built on piles that raised them above the damp or

---

Mound Builders

A term used for Native Americans who built various types of earth mound for burial and ceremonial purposes.

Curriculum Context

Students learning about the social and political structure of major Pre-Contact groups, might choose to focus on the hierarchical organization of the Mississippian mound-building cultures.

swampy ground or were cool, open-sided chickee huts. The people practiced a great deal of farming and fishing, with the rich forests, swamps, and saltwater marshes providing all kinds of game for hunters. Harvests and associated festivals were the centerpiece of the ritual year, notably the Green Corn ceremonies and dances.

European contact

Warfare to force compliance and assert dominance was common, so there was resistance to settlement and conquest. But the European pressure—from all the major powers over time: Britain, France, Spain, and then the new United States—coupled with the terrible epidemics of disease, resulted in the decimation of the tribes.

Curriculum Context

As part of a study of Jackson's presidency, the curriculum might ask students to describe the policy of Indian removal and its impact on Native American groups such as the Cherokee.

Forced relocation

The defining event for the tribes was President Andrew Jackson's policy of forced relocation following his Indian Removal Act of 1830—the infamous Trail of Tears. One-quarter of all Cherokee died during this march over hundreds of miles of harsh terrain.

Struggle for survival

Even so, small groups managed to resist the policy and remain in their homelands, such as the eastern Cherokee of Qualla reservation in the Great Smoky Mountains. However, most of their descendants now live in Oklahoma, their culture massively diminished.

Timucua

The Timucua people lived in eastern Florida. The Spanish conquistador, or conqueror, Juan Ponce de León was the first European to make contact with them following his landfall in Florida in 1513. The Timucua lived in palisaded, or fenced, villages ruled over by privileged chiefs who maintained a social hierarchy and collected tribute from their domain.

At the time of European contact, the Native American population of this part of the Southeast was large, well structured, and hostile. Besides the Timucua, the warlike Calusa lived in the Everglades, the Apalachee in western Florida, and the Ais and Tequesta between these regions. Warfare to force compliance and assert dominance was common.

Armed resistance

In 1521 Ponce de León returned to Florida with missionaries, intent on forcing the local Native Americans to convert to Christianity. Spanish forays greatly provoked the Timucua, Calusa, and Apalachee, who resisted the Europeans fiercely. Ponce de León himself died of a wound inflicted by a poisoned dart fired from a Calusa blow-pipe.

The Spanish did not give up, however, and another conquistador, Hernando de Soto, took up the cause. He cemented a relationship with the Timucua through a Spaniard who was living among them, having fled captivity from the Calusa, and had learned their language. This fortunate connection meant de Soto had local scouts and knowledge. His force cut a swathe through the peoples of the Southeast, trailing death and destruction.

In the decades that followed, the Spanish built settlements and forts, and Franciscan missionaries

Curriculum Context

Students learning about the motives of early European explorers might choose to focus on the role of religion in the expeditions of the Spanish conquistadors.

This coloured engraving shows the Spanish conquistador Hernando de Soto and his men torturing Native Americans in Florida.

moved among the Timucua and other Florida tribes. About 1650 the Franciscans estimated the Timucua to number 10,000, with thousands more speaking their language in other related tribes.

Victims of European settlement

Unfortunately for the Florida tribes their territories became the battleground for European powers competing for the spoils of a new continent. The Spanish controlled the region until 1763, when the British acquired Florida. The few remaining converted Timucua fled with the Spanish. The more powerful Creek, allied to the British, moved into their territory.

It is thought that the remaining Timucua and other victims of European settlement in Florida, such as the Yamasee, eventually merged into the Mikasuki and then the Seminole—so wiping out the Timucua as a distinct people.

Curriculum Context

The population of the Timucua declined rapidly after European contact and by the time the U.S. acquired Florida in 1821 they no longer existed as a distinct group.

Upper Missouri Tribes

Originally, Plains peoples were farmers and lived in semipermanent settlements along the Upper Missouri River in modern-day North Dakota. The introduction of horses in the 16th century created a new, nomadic way of life for peoples. Those groups that remained in semipermanent settlements formed a subgroup of the Plains culture—the Upper Missouri tribal region.

The Upper Missouri tribes divide into two language groups: the Siouan-speaking Mandan and Hidatsa, and the Caddoan-speaking Arikara.

The Mandan lifestyle

Probably the most influential Upper Missouri tribe was the Mandan. They grew corn, beans, squash, and sunflowers and hunted buffalo and elk. During the spring and summer they fished. They lived in villages of semiunderground earth lodges. Each village was surrounded by a defensive palisade (a fence of stakes).

Curriculum Context

In a comparative study of the lifestyles of Pre-Contact groups, students might focus on the way in which the Mandan obtained their food and the type of homes they built.

This 1908 photograph shows a Mandan earthen lodge. Early lodges were rectangular, though the Mandan started building circular loges about 1500.

Curriculum Context

The curriculum might ask students to explore the impact of European diseases on native groups. The epidemic of 1837 reduced the Mandan population to around 125.

When a French fur-trade expedition encountered the Mandan in 1738, the tribe was living in nine villages situated hundreds of miles apart along the bank of the Missouri River. Each settlement was made up of several dozen households arranged on terraced land.

A smallpox epidemic in 1781 reduced the Mandan population severely; and when Lewis and Clark visited the Mandan in 1804, only two villages were left. A second smallpox epidemic in 1837 almost wiped the group out.

A trading people

The tribes of the Upper Missouri were a focal point of an intertribal trading network in which the Mandan, Hidatsa, and Arikara were middlemen. The acquisition of guns and horses in particular marked the birth of "traditional" Plains culture, the heyday of which lasted from about 1800 to 1870.

This map shows the homelands of the Hidatsa, Mandan, and Arikara and the location of neighboring Native American groups.

Rituals and beliefs

The Upper Missouri tribes believed deeply in the mystery and power of nature. They derived great strength from supernatural visions and from celebrating and praising the natural world in rituals such as the Mandan Okipa ritual. This ceremony dramatized the creation of the Earth, its people, animals, and plants, and symbolically renewed the world for another year. The Okipa was performed every summer. The Mandan believed that, by performing the ceremony regularly, they would guarantee plentiful buffalo herds and good fortune for the coming year.

Other Upper Missouri tribes

The Hidatsa were a seminomadic people. They learned to grow corn from the Mandan and farmed the Upper Missouri region of North Dakota. They were the best known native tobacco growers and were deeply involved in the gun and horse trades.

Farther south the Arikara were the trading link to the Cheyenne and Teton Sioux. Early French fur traders identified the Arikara settlement at the Grand River as a good place to access the Plains trade network and obtain furs and pelts. However, smallpox and conflict with the Sioux took a heavy toll on the Arikara.

The Three Affiliated Tribes

After the 1837 smallpox epidemic, survivors from the Mandan and Hidatsa joined together at Fort Berthold reservation, North Dakota, in 1845. They were joined there in 1862 by the Arikara, whose population had been halved by smallpox, and formed the Three Affiliated Tribes. By then, developments that had taken place during the growth of the fur trade had eroded the groups' preeminence as trading centers. European contact had been devastating for the groups in terms of both disease and commerce.

Glossary

American Indian Movement (AIM)
A civil rights organization that seeks the restoration of original tribal lands and better treatment of Native Americans.

Battle of Little Bighorn A battle that took place in the valley of the Little Bighorn River, Montana, in June 1876. Lieutenant Colonel George Custer and his forces suffered a crushing defeat by Sioux, Cheyenne, and Arapaho warriors.

Chickee A Seminole house built on stilts, with a log frame, open sides, and a thatched roof over a raised wooden platform. *Chickee* is the Seminole word for house.

Clan A social unit consisting of a number of households or families with a common ancestor.

Confederacy A league or alliance. Native American confederacies often included several united tribes or bands which formed an association to support one another.

Counting coup Among Plains peoples, an act of bravery in battle involving striking a blow against an enemy warrior's body with a decorated stick. The acts were recorded by making notches in the coup stick or by adding a feather to the warrior's headdress.

Dawes General Allotment Act A U.S. law passed in 1887 to divide up reservation lands and provide individual Native American households with an allotment of land to farm.

French and Indian War A war (1754–1763) fought between Britain and France and their respective Native American allies for colonial supremacy in North America. British victory was confirmed in the Treaty of Paris in 1763.

Ghost Dance Native American religious movement of the late 19th century that involved the performance of a ritual dance in order to bring an end to the westward expansion of white settlers and restore Native American land and traditional tribal life.

Great Law of Peace A set of laws recorded on a series of wampum belts, laying down the founding constitution of the Iroquois League.

Hudson's Bay Company A trading company set up in 1670 in the Hudson Bay area of North America. It controlled the fur trade in the region for centuries, forming a network of trading posts and obtaining fur from local peoples in exchange for goods shipped from Britain.

Indian Removal Act A federal law signed by President Andrew Jackson in 1830 authorizing the removal of Native Americans from their lands in the east and their resettlement in the west.

Indian Reorganization Act Legislation passed June 18, 1934, also known as the Indian New Deal. It attempted to give new rights to Native Americans living on reservations, reversing the Dawes General Allotment Act and restoring self-government on a tribal basis.

Indian Territory Land mainly in present-day Oklahoma set aside in 1834 for Native Americans who had been forced to leave their homelands. The Indian Territory was dissolved when Oklahoma became a state in 1907.

Longhouse A communal house shared by several families. Longhouses measured up to 200 feet (60 m) in length and were built of post frames covered in bark.

Louisiana Purchase The purchase by the United States from France in 1803 of 828,000 square miles (2,144,000 sq km) of land, comprising the western part of the Mississippi valley, including the modern-day states of Louisiana, Missouri, Arkansas, Iowa, Nebraska, North Dakota, South Dakota, and Oklahoma.

Medicine Lodge Treaty A set of three treaties signed in 1867 at Medicine Lodge Creek, Kansas, between the U.S. government and the Kiowa, Comanche, Plains Apache, Southern Cheyenne, and Arapaho. The treaties involved the surrender of tribal homelands in exchange for reservations in the Indian Territory.

Mound Builders A term used for Native Americans who built various types of earth mound for burial and ceremonial purposes.

Pequot War A conflict in 1636–1637 between an alliance of English colonists and the Mohegan and Narragansett against the Pequot under their chief, Sassacus. The conflict resulted in the defeat of the Pequot.

Powwow A gathering of Native Americans, often involving feasting and dancing. The word comes from the Narragansett word *powwaw*, meaning "shaman" or "magician."

Pueblo peoples Native American village-dwelling peoples of the Southwest, including modern-day New Mexico and Arizona.

Roach A hairstyle in which the head is shaved except for a strip from front to back across the top of the head.

Shaman A person regarded as having special powers to access the spirit world and an ability to use magic to heal the sick and control events.

Sun Dance An important ceremony practiced by Plains peoples to celebrate the renewal of nature.

Tepee A cone-shaped tent built with a pole framework traditionally covered with animal skins.

Trail of Tears A term used to describe the relocation Cherokee and other Native Americans from their homelands to the Indian Territory. The forced march led to the deaths of around 4,000 Cherokee.

Vision Quest A rite of passage in many Native American groups, in which young individuals go alone to an isolated place to seek protection from the spirits.

Wampum belt A decorative belt consisting of small cylindrical beads made from polished shells. The belts were used for ceremonial purposes and to record important events.

War of 1812 A war (1812–1815) between the United States and Britain over trade restrictions introduced by Britain to impede U.S. trade with France. The war ended with the Treaty of Ghent and neither side was victorious.

Wattle-and-daub A building material traditionally used for making walls and consisting of an interwoven lattice of wooden sticks, covered with a material such as clay.

Wigwam A domed dwelling consisting of a single room, formed on a frame of arched poles and covered with a roofing material such as birchbark, grass, or hides.

Further Research

BOOKS

Basel, Roberta. *Sequoyah: Inventor of Written Cherokee*, "Signature Lives" series. Compass Point Books, 2008.

Behrman, Carol H. *The Indian Wars*, "Chronicles of America's Wars" series. Lerner Publications, 2004.

Blaisdell, Bob (ed.). *Great Speeches by Native Americans*. Dover Publications, 2000.

Bowes, John P. *The Trail of Tears: Removal in the South*, "Landmark Events in Native American History" series. Chelsea House Publications, 2007.

Doherty, Craig A., and Katherine M. Doherty. *Northeast Indians*. Chelsea House Publications, 2008.

Dunn, John M. *The Relocation of the North American Indian*, "World History" series. Lucent Books, 2005.

Haugen, Brenda. *Crazy Horse: Sioux Warrior*, "Signature Lives" series. Compass Point Books,2006.

Hinshaw Patent, Dorothy. *The Buffalo and the Indians: A Shared Destiny*. Clarion Books, 2006.

Johnson, Michael. *Encyclopedia of Native Tribes of North America*. Firefly Books, 2007.

Lawson, Michael L. *Little Bighorn: Winning the Battle, Losing the War*, "Landmark Events in Native American History" series. Chelsea House Publications, 2007.

Milner, George R. *The Moundbuilders: Ancient Peoples of Eastern North America*. Thames & Hudson, 2005.

Philip, Neil. *The Great Circle: A History of the First Nations*. Clarion Books, 2006.

Pritzker, Barry M. *A Native American Encyclopedia: History, Culture, and Peoples*. Oxford University Press, 2000.

Roop, Peter, and Connie Roop. *Sitting Bull*. Scholastic, 2002.

Sturgis, Amy H. *Tecumseh: A Biography*. Greenwood Press, 2008.

Waldman, Carl, and Molly Braun. *Encyclopedia of Native American Tribes*. Facts on File, third edition, 2006.

Wilcox, Charlotte. *The Iroquois*, "Native American Histories" series. Lerner Publications, 2006.

INTERNET RESOURCES

NativeAmericans.com. A comprehensive site with information about all aspects of Native American history, including online biographies, extensive bibliographies, and information about the culture of Native American groups.
www.nativeamericans.com

Smithsonian: American Indian History and Culture. A Smithsonian Institution website, with information about all aspects of Native American history and culture.
www.si.edu/Encyclopedia_SI/History_and_Culture/AmericanIndian_History.htm

National Museum of the American Indian. This Smithsonian Institution website provides information about the collections of the National Museum of the American Indian as well as educational resources for students about the history and culture of Native Americans.
www.nmai.si.edu/

American Indian Tribal/Nation Home Pages. A University of Oklahoma website, with links to the home pages of Native American peoples.
www.law.ou.edu/native/ainations.shtml

NativeWeb. A website with links to all aspects of Native American studies.
www.nativeweb.org/

First Nations Histories. Provides an overview of the histories of Native American groups as well as a location list of native peoples in the United States and Canada.
www.tolatsga.org/Compacts.html

Native Americans Documents Project. Provides access to documents relating to Native American history, including federal Indian policy and the Dawes General Allotment Act.
www2.csusm.edu/nadp/

Native American History. Site from the University of Washington, with links to information on all aspects of Native American history.
www.lib.washington.edu/subject/history/tm/native.html

The Plains Indians. A website providing information about the Plains Native Americans.
http://inkido.indiana.edu/w310work/romac/plains.html

Seminole History. Information on the history of the Seminole people of Florida, from the Florida Department of State.
www.flheritage.com/facts/history/seminole/

Index

Page numbers in *italic* refer to illustrations.

Upper Missouri tribes 105
see also spirits
reservations *see* Dawes General
   Allotment Act; Indian Removal
   Act; Indian Territory; Trail of
   Tears
rituals
   death rituals 74
   Five Civilized Tribes 50
   Iroquois 59
   Mandan Okipa 105
   Pawnee 85
   renewal 16, 28, 30, 105
   Southeast/Florida peoples 100
   Sun Dance 16, 19, 27, 29–30, 43
   Upper Missouri tribes 105
   Vision Quest 29, 43, 97
   warfare 17
   see also ceremonies

Sacred Bundles 85
sacrifices 66, 67, 74
Sand Creek Massacre 12, 31
Sauk and Fox 78, 86–87, *87*, 93
Sassacus (Pequot chief) 71
scalping 18, 96
Seminole *52*, 88–92, *89*, *91*, 99,
   102
   see also Five Civilized Tribes;
      Southeast/Florida peoples
Seminole wars 89–92, *91*
Seneca 57–61, *60*, 68
Sequoyah 25, *25*, 52
Serpent Mound, Ohio 7
shamans 28, 36, 47, 59, 86
Shawnee 79, 93–94
Shoshoni 19, 32
Sioux 13, 14, 20, 27, 31, 37, 43,
   78, 84, 95–98, *98*
   Wounded Knee 13, 98
Sitting Bull 13, 20, 97, 98
slaves 50, 66, 75, 88, 89
smallpox 14, 20, 40, 55–56, 71,
   84, 104, 105
   see also diseases; epidemics
Soto, Hernando de 67, 72, *72*, 73,
   99, 101, *102*
Southeast/Florida peoples
   99–100
   see also Five Civilized Tribes;
      Mississippians
Southern Cheyenne 12
Southern Cult 65, 66–67, *66*
spirits 19, 23, 29–30, 47, 59, 96,
   97, 105
   see also Sun Dance; Vision
      Quest
Sun Dance 16, 19, 27, 29–30, *30*,
   43
sweat lodge 19

tattoos 39, 73, 80
Tecumseh 79, 93–94, *94*
Temple Mound Builders 65–67,
   72
Tenskwataw 93
tepees 11, *11*, 18, 27, 38, 42, 80,
   83, 95
Teton Sioux 95, 105
Thadodaho 59
Thames, Battle of the 94, *94*
Thayendaneken (Mohawk chief)
   68, 69, *69*
Three Affiliated Tribes 105
Timucua 101–102
Tippecanoe 94
tobacco 43, 46, 50, 59, 72, 95, 97,
   105
tourism 26, 35
towns 54, 99
   see also Five Civilized Tribes
trade
   between Native American
      groups 7, 8, 11, 33, 38, 47,
      95, 104
   fur 8, 9, 10, 14–15, 19, 38, 39,
      47, 56, 61, 78, 80, 104, 105
   guns 39, 61, 78, 80, 95, 104
   horses 11, 43, 80, 95, 104, 105
   Hudson's Bay Company 11, 14,
      19, 39–40
   with settlers 8, *8*, 14–15, 19,
      24, 38–39, 43, 61, 74, 78, 80
Trail of Tears 25–26, 90, 100
treaties 14, 15, 20, 32, 48, 83
   Council Springs 23
   Fort Laramie 30, 44, 97
   Ghent 94
   Medicine Lodge 12, 13, 34
tribal societies 16, 17, 19, 28, 78
tribute 99, 101
Turkey Dance 23
Tuscarora 57

U.S. Constitution 61
Uamasee 88
Uncas (Mohegan chief) 71
Union of New Brunswick Indians
   64
Union of Nova Scotia Indians 64
United Keetoowah Band of
   Oklahoma 26
Upper Missouri tribes 14,
   103–105

Verrazano, Giovanni da 47
Vision Quest 29, 43, 97
Vizenor, Gerald 79

wampum belt 59, 60
War of 1812 53, 94

warrior societies 16, 17, 28–29
West, Sir Thomas 45
wigwam 62, *63*
Winnebago 86
women *13*, 18, 22, 28, 42, 46, 50,
   54–55, 58, 60, 64
Wounded Knee 13, 98
Wyandots 56

Yankton Sioux 95
Young Dog Dance 85
Yuchi 88